a healthier home
COOK

Quarto.com

© 2024 Quarto Publishing Group USA Inc.

Text © 2024 Shawna Holman

First Published in 2024 by Fair Winds Press, an imprint of The Quarto Group,
100 Cummings Center, Suite 265-D, Beverly, MA 01915, USA.
T (978) 282-9590 F (978) 283-2742

Fair Winds Press titles are also available at discount for retail, wholesale, promotional, and bulk purchase. For details, contact the Special Sales Manager by email at specialsales@quarto.com or by mail at The Quarto Group, Attn: Special Sales Manager, 100 Cummings Center, Suite 265-D, Beverly, MA 01915, USA.

28 27 26 25 24   1 2 3 4 5

ISBN: 978-0-7603-8865-5

Digital edition published in 2024
eISBN: 978-0-7603-8866-2

Library of Congress Cataloging-in-Publication Data

Names: Holman, Shawna, author.
Title: A healthier home cook : whole food recipes, techniques, and tips for
   families that want to eat a little less toxic / Shawna Holman.
Description: Beverly, MA, USA : Fair Winds Press, an imprint of The Quarto
   Group, 2024. | Includes index. | Summary: "With A Healthier Home Cook as
   your accessible guide, set up your kitchen with an eye toward removing
   toxins, then cook your way through 75+ wholesome recipes"-- Provided by
   publisher.
Identifiers: LCCN 2024016195 | ISBN 9780760388655 | ISBN 9780760388662
   (ebook)
Subjects: LCSH: Cooking. | LCGFT: Cookbooks.
Classification: LCC TX714 .H6465 2024 | DDC 641.5--dc23/eng/20240429
LC record available at https://lccn.loc.gov/2024016195

Cover Image: Monica Stevens Le

Page Layout: *tabula rasa* graphic design

Photography: Monica Stevens Le, except Kayla Mangione and Jillian Scarpetti on pages 138, 140, and 150

Printed in China

a healthier home
COOK

Whole-Food Recipes,
Techniques, and Tips for
Families That Want to Eat
A LITTLE LESS TOXIC®

Shawna Holman

FAIR WINDS

Contents

Introduction

The first time I *enjoyed* a plain almond as an adult, okay as a thirtysomething-year-old adult, it blew my mind. I'd had almonds countless times before, of course, but they always tasted bland and felt unpleasant. After I committed to eating only ingredients I understood—the ones found in nature that made me feel so good—things changed fast. Soon, a silly little almond left me in awe.

What changed? I realized that I had been held captive by the tactics of an industry that wants my money, and it had robbed me of enjoying real food. Without the distractions and biological manipulation of the highly processed foods, I was so thrilled to appreciate, celebrate, and thoroughly relish textures and subtle flavors as I never had before. I had always loved food, just not this way. It took breaking the grip the lab-manufactured foods had on me and my body coming back into better balance to be able to enjoy real, pure, whole foods. Over the years that followed, it became my mission to re-create some of my longtime favorites from when I was under the deception of Big Food, but make them with ingredients that taste amazing and help you feel great too.

Feelings and Food

For me, food is not neutral. Food is powerful, and it can support health or impede it. I know there is a push from some to neutralize feelings and beliefs around foods. I just can't get on board with this concept. I never want to demonize food, and I want all people to be fed. I'm not advocating for "good food versus bad food." However, I also want to be more than fed. I want people to understand how to be well nourished. Restricting isn't nourishing. Bingeing isn't nourishing. Fear isn't nourishing. Shame isn't nourishing. It's also not healthy or nourishing to believe that a highly processed food item loaded with sugar is somehow equal to a piece of fresh fruit. What is nourishing is having a healthy view of food and using food to help support the body.

It's important to have understanding and wisdom around how we nourish and fuel ourselves. I want more people to have a healthy view of food. I believe that involves seeing food with discernment plus gratitude and awe. Understanding the effect that food, as it was intended, can have on our minds, bodies, and well-being is part of this. Some foods contribute to balance and healing, while others impede and even derail health. Just as I would be mindful about the type of fuel I put in a fancy race car, I want to be intentional about the fuel I put in the much more valuable "machine" that is my body.

Food is so much more than fuel, too. Food is also tradition, nostalgia, fellowship, community, culture, memories, communication with the body, fun, and more. I believe everyone can make nourishing things that are delicious, nostalgic, and fun without all the highly processed ingredients.

Back to Basics

Not more than three generations ago, most food was organic and untouched by modern pesticides. Virtually all food was made from scratch by the hands of someone who cared for you. Even store-bought food was made using real food ingredients. Animals used for milk, meat, and eggs were raised outdoors, moving their bodies, on pastures, in the sunshine, consuming the diets they have for all of their history. After desperation and shortages during major wars, the industrial revolution, and the growth of the food industry, which was more and more monopolized by just a handful of corporations over time, food changed drastically. The grocery store today is a very different place than it once was, and you have to fill your kitchen and body intentionally by reading labels and doing research.

It's possible to do this though, and I believe it's time to take back control. Our taste buds and minds have been manipulated and taken captive by marketing, highly manufactured ingredients, and food products crafted with the intention of making people crave them and grow insatiable desires for more of the same. It's time we get back to the basics.

Our taste buds, cravings, and even our bodies and minds have been reshaped and hijacked to think these highly processed foods taste better, and foods in their pure form taste almost bland in comparison. Maybe you are already on this journey, but if not, the first step is to reset your body and mind. In a relatively short amount of time, once you remove the trickster foods, you can and will retrain your mind, body, and palate to appreciate real food. My hope is that you, too, are able to have a simple "almond" moment, when you realize how delicious real food can be.

Chapter 1

Welcome to the
A Little Less Toxic
Kitchen

What I Use to Cook

You probably already have a well-stocked kitchen. I don't want you to go in there and throw out everything you have and break the bank making it a professional, restaurant-level, perfectly nontoxic wonderland. The most important thing is to make more food at home with your own hands. Using what you already have is a perfect place to start. Then, as something wears out or runs out, this chapter will be here to help you find a healthier replacement that hopefully will fit your needs and budget.

Pots and Pans

While many nonstick coatings claim to be less toxic or nontoxic, there really aren't any I'd consider using in my kitchen. In addition to that, those surfaces wear out faster and I'd challenge you to find a nonstick pan that lasts as many years as good-quality stainless steel or cast iron. A quality set of stainless steel pans will last an entire lifetime (or longer) with minimal care. There is a small learning curve, but with a few attempts following some basic principles you can cook anything and everything easily in your stainless steel pots and pans—and you'll cook better and have healthier outcomes for your food, the air, and the people you feed.

My suggestion is to invest in stainless steel pots and pans that have a good heat conductor at the core, such as aluminum. Aluminum is not nontoxic, so I want my pots and pans to have a solid covering over that. I suggest three-ply to five-ply clad, and I prefer to have that not just on the base of the pan but all the way up the sides, inside and out. Aluminum will allow the pans to heat well and evenly and hold that temperature appropriately, while the stainless steel provides a great barrier between that and your food. My preference for stainless steel is 18/10. This indicates the chromium to nickel ratio. Nickel isn't completely nontoxic, so it's important it is no higher than 10. However, nickel prevents corrosion, rust, and stains, so it's important to have in your stainless steel so your pots and pans last. I would not go lower than 18/10, personally (18/8 will not retain its polished appearance long and 18/0 will rust and corrode too easily).

Tip: Unless you're trying to reach a boil, you virtually never need to heat stainless steel pans above medium. Doing so will cause foods to stick and burn. Also, let these pans heat up several minutes before using. This allows the pores at the surface to get smaller, creating a slicker, more naturally low-stick surface. If you're not sure if it's ready, sprinkle in a few drops of water. If it hisses and splutters, your pan isn't ready. If it beads up and dances around looking a bit like mercury beads, you're good to go.

Cast Iron

The cast-iron pan is the most used piece of equipment in my kitchen. This multipurpose workhorse is great for everything from pancakes to eggs to veggies to steaks. It's really a time-honored, all-purpose beast. This is another pan that with a little care will last a lifetime, or even generations!

Cast-Iron Tips: Most pans are preseasoned with oils I prefer not to use. It's not a deal-breaker for me though: Eventually the oils will wash

away, but it can take time because the pans are seasoned with oils intended to penetrate the surface and into the pores. To remedy this at home, give the pan a good scrub and start the seasoning process over again.

Some use soap to clean their cast-iron pans without issue. I prefer to skip soaps and retain all those layers of "seasoning" when possible. I can't recall the last time I found the use of soap necessary.

Avoid These Materials

Nonstick: Contains substances such as PFAS (polyfluorinated substances) linked to many ailments and diseases including effects to reproduction, thyroid function, and the immune system.

Plastic: Contains components such as BPA, BPF, and BPS linked to developmental, reproductive, and systemic toxicity. Microplastics are continually being found in the water supply and even bloodstream. Plastic degrades and can contaminate foods, especially with heat.

Aluminum (with direct contact to food): Neurotoxic and linked to health issues including Alzheimer's disease.

Microwave: Potential radiation exposure, especially with older units and any with worn or faulty seals.

Glues: Items that are held together by glue (e.g., a wood handle with a silicone spatula, bamboo cutting boards, etc.). Openings are traps for moisture and allow bacteria and mold to form. The adhesives themselves are also potentially toxic and will get into your food and air, especially over time.

To Use: Low and medium heat are best when cooking most things with cast iron. Also, avoid cooking with acidic ingredients that increase iron leaching into food (e.g., lemon, tomato, vinegar, etc.). Use good fats to grease the pan, as needed.

To Clean: Wipe out and use very hot water and stainless steel chain mail or a very stiff brush to remove any residue or caked on materials. Dry thoroughly.

I like to heat my pan up on the stove after cleaning to ensure thorough drying and to open those pores at the surface a bit. I take a clean cloth or paper towel and rub a very small amount of coconut oil all over while the pan is still warm. Allow the pan to cool before storing it, and store it in a cool, dry place.

Bakeware

Glass and ceramic are my top choices for casserole dishes, loaf pans, and the like. For muffin tins and baking sheets, I want to caution you from wasting money on pieces that are 100 percent stainless steel. It just doesn't conduct heat well enough. If you cannot afford to buy bakeware that is stainless-steel clad over aluminum core, as these pieces are often very pricey, my recommendation is to use what you have and line it with unbleached parchment paper.

My Handy Kitchen Tools Replacement Chart

Item	Conventional	A Little Less Toxic Option 1	A Little Less Toxic Option 2
Pans	Nonstick	Ceramic coated without PFOA or PFAS	18/10 fully clad stainless-steel pots and pans, cast-iron skillet and griddle pan
Bakeware	Nonstick, aluminum	Lining with unbleached parchment paper	Glass, ceramic, or fully clad stainless steel with aluminum core
Set and Forget	Slow cooker (many found to contain lead)	Lead-free slow cooker	Stainless steel slow cooker or pressure cooker
Cutting Boards	Plastic	Bamboo (many smaller pieces held together with glues)	Solid wood
Heating Appliances	Microwave and nonstick air fryers	Stainless steel toaster oven (if convection it will air-fry) or pressure cooker	
Cooking Utensils	Plastic spoons and spatulas, aluminum turner	Bamboo and utensils that are two pieces— silicone glued to bamboo or wood	Solid wood, stainless steel, and solid silicone
Mixing Bowls, Measuring Cups, etc.	Plastic	Glass, stainless, silicone, solid wood (no glues)	
Storage Containers	Plastic	Glass, stainless, silicone	
Baking Liners and Food Storage Wrap	Plastic, aluminum foil	Silicone, unbleached parchment paper, beeswax	

A Few Notes on Parchment Paper

Parchment paper is less toxic than aluminum, and using unbleached parchment paper reduces exposure to toxins such as dioxin. If you're just getting started, here are a few tips. First, crumple your sheet of parchment paper in your hands into a ball. This makes it lay down flat on or in your bakeware. If you really need to use an aluminum surface for cooking, such as frying in an aluminum pan, covering a dish with foil to bake, or grilling corn on the cob wrapped in foil, add a layer of parchment paper between your food and the aluminum to reduce toxic exposure, especially when using heat.

Cutting Boards

As you use your plastic cutting board, plastic will get into your food, especially as you run a knife blade against it over and over. Plastic cutting boards also tend to dull your knives more quickly than wood. Bamboo is a better choice for the longevity of your knives as well as your health and the health of the planet, but it is held together with adhesives that aren't great for health. Opt for solid pieces of wood when possible. Wood is naturally antimicrobial, won't dull your knives, and is naturally nontoxic.

Utensils

Buy stainless steel, glass, silicone, and solid wood versions for things such as graters, measuring cups, mixing bowls, and measuring spoons.

Food Storage

Glass food storage containers are fairly low-cost in sets, and they frequently go on sale. Repurposing glass jars is another option to avoid plastic. Glass canning jars, such as mason jars, can be used with hot or cold foods, and they even work great for freezing items if you leave space for expansion and shift temperature gradually. Silicone storage bags work well for times where you really want plastic portability. Instead of foil, I like unbleached parchment paper, clean flour-sack towels, or beeswax to cover bowls without lids.

Other Kitchen Tools

You absolutely do not need high-end equipment to make food at home. If you don't have all the fancy gadgets, remember, our great grandmas did virtually everything with a wooden spoon and a whisk. You've got this. That said, here are the things I use a ton that I think are worth the investment whenever you can make it:

- A good, sharp set of knives. You probably don't need more than a chef's knife, a paring knife, and a serrated bread knife, but a carving knife and second chopping knife can come in handy.

- Blender

- Electric pressure cooker

- Dutch oven

- Stainless steel colander as well as a fine-mesh stainless-steel strainer

- Silicone spoonula for mixing and scooping

- Three sizes of stainless-steel ice cream scoopers. These are great for making muffins, cookies, rice balls, meatballs, and so much more

- Garlic press (stainless steel)

- Citrus squeezer or reamer (stainless steel)

- Whisk (stainless steel)

- Tongs

- Meat thermometer

- Microplane

- Box grater

- Vegetable peeler

- Can opener

- Mortar and pestle

- Silicone spatulas

Nonessential but sure are helpful:

- Immersion blender

- Food processor

- Hand mixer or stand mixer

- Coffee grinder

- Batter bowl. This is not necessary, but I use mine multiple times a day, every day.

The Pantry

Keeping a well-stocked pantry helps me put together a nourishing meal with little prep, and it makes it easier to cook more meals at home and eat out less.

Salts, Sweeteners, Fats, and Acids

- Oils and fats: Extra-virgin olive oil, unrefined virgin or extra-virgin coconut oil, avocado oil, tallow, ghee, toasted sesame oil

- Acids: Unpasteurized apple cider vinegar, red wine vinegar, white wine vinegar, aged balsamic vinegar, rice vinegar

- Sweeteners: Raw honey, pure grade B maple syrup, dried dates, coconut sugar, unsulfured molasses, dried or fresh fruits

Dried and Canned/Jarred Goods

- Seeds, legumes, grains, and nuts: Chia, hemp, flax, quinoa, and pumpkin seeds. Raw and plain nuts (e.g., almonds, Brazil nuts, cashews, macadamia nuts, pine nuts, pecans, and walnuts). Organic groats or rolled or steel-cut oats without added ingredients. Dried legumes and beans (e.g., split peas; lentils; black, pinto, kidney, cannellini, and adzuki beans). Nut butters made with organic, raw nuts or seeds and no added ingredients.

- Meats and seafood: Pasture-raised, grass-fed jerky. Pasture-raised poultry in cans or jars. Wild-caught sardines, salmon, tuna, oysters, anchovies.

- Dried medicinal berries and herbs: Goji berry, star anise, cloves, kombu

- Collagen and gelatin powders from pasture-raised, grass-fed cows

- Dry pasta with minimal and whole-food ingredients

- Treats: Fair trade organic dark chocolate (at least 70% cacao)

Condiments

- Organic ketchup with only organic sugar or no added sugars

- Mustard without oils, sugars, or other additives

- Mayonnaise made with avocado, coconut, or olive oil and whole-food ingredients

- Coconut aminos: a great alternative to soy sauce, especially for those like me who don't tolerate soy very well

- Fish sauce without sugar, MSG, or preservatives. (The ingredients list should be just anchovies and sea salt.)

- Worcestershire sauce without natural flavorings or other mystery ingredients

- Tahini with sesame seeds as the only ingredient

- Hot sauces with only whole-food ingredients

I make my salad dressings and marinades myself as I find it fun, easy, and a big-time money saver. If you want to keep store-bought versions in your pantry for convenience, look for ones with whole-food ingredients that use better oils (e.g., olive, avocado, or coconut) and without artificial sweeteners or mystery ingredients such as "natural flavors" or "artificial flavors."

Herbs and Seasonings

No kitchen is complete without basic salt and pepper. Let's make it good-quality, unrefined sea salt without anticaking agents or any other added ingredients. Common table salts sometimes even have sugar hiding in there. In addition to those two staples, a well-stocked pantry should have other essential seasonings. These can make a boring dish special, plus herbs and spices can contain ample vitamins and minerals and have numerous health benefits. I'll list a few for each of my pantry must-haves.

continued on page 20

My Handy Shopping Chart

Avoid	A Little Less Toxic Option 1	A Little Less Toxic Option 2
Dyes (e.g., Blue 1, Red 3, Red 40, Yellow 5, Yellow 6)	Foods colored with real food (e.g., beet powder, turmeric, blue spirulina, freeze-dried carrots)	
Artificial flavors	No artificial flavors, but maybe (some) "natural flavors" on the list	Full ingredient transparency; no mystery ingredients
Ultra-processed oils that can be more inflammatory (e.g., canola, vegetable, soybean, rapeseed, butter alternatives with hydrogenated oils)	Butter, ghee, animal fats, cold-pressed olive oil, coconut oil, avocado oil	
Artificial sweeteners (e.g., sucralose, aspartame, erythritol, high-fructose corn syrup)	Cane sugar	Maple syrup, raw honey, coconut sugar, dates, monk fruit
MSG	Table salt	Sea salt
Toxic preservatives (e.g., synthetic nitrates, BHA/BHT, calcium propionate, sodium benzoate/benzoic acid)	More natural preservatives (e.g., ascorbic acid, [non-mold] citric acid, vitamin E [tocopherols])	Avoid foods that require preservatives or are preserved with methods such as freezing, canning, pickling, and fermenting.
Dairy alternatives with unnecessary ingredients	Store-bought dairy alternatives with only real food ingredients (only nuts/seeds/oats, water, salt, vanilla)	Homemade nut, seed, oat milks
Conventional dairy; cows in concentrated animal farming operations	Grass-fed A2 dairy; low-pasteurized, grass-fed dairy	Ultra-low-pasteurized A2 dairy; raw, nonhomogenized dairy from animals raised on pasture
Conventional eggs and poultry: raised in overcrowded hen houses; low to no outdoor access; fed on GMO grain	"Free range" and organic	Pasture-raised; even better if pasture-raised and the supplement given is organic

Avoid	A Little Less Toxic Option 1	A Little Less Toxic Option 2
CAFO (concentrated animal farming operation) meats	Grass-fed, organic	Pasture-raised; grass-fed and grass-finished; any supplement is organic
Farm-raised fish; dyed fish (common with farm-raised salmon)	Wild-caught	Wild-caught; low-mercury fish (e.g., salmon, sardines, anchovies, Arctic cod)

- Basil: Anti-inflammatory, antioxidant, heart health, liver and immune support, antibacterial

- Cayenne and other hot peppers: Circulatory support, antioxidants, cell health, digestive support, heart health

- Ceylon cinnamon: Antimicrobial, circulatory health, anti-inflammatory, blood sugar regulation, eye health, cholesterol support

- Coriander: Antioxidants, blood sugar regulation, heart health, antibacterial, detoxifying

- Cumin: Immune support, digestive health, antioxidants, anticancer properties

- Garlic: Heart health, blood pressure support, healthy cholesterol, sugar regulation support, immune health

- Ginger: Anti-inflammatory, digestive support

- Mustard: Antioxidant, nervous system support, respiratory health

- Onion: Supports healthy blood pressure and blood sugar levels, antioxidants, enzymes that help support digestion, heart health

- Oregano: Antimicrobial, antioxidant, antiviral, anti-inflammatory

- Paprika: Eye health, anti-inflammatory, blood sugar– and cholesterol-regulating properties

- Parsley: Antioxidant; antibacterial; bone, eye, and heart health support

- Rosemary: Antioxidants, mood support, antimicrobial, digestion

- Sage: Anti-inflammatory, antioxidant, brain support

- Thyme: Antibacterial, antioxidant, lung health

- Turmeric: Anti-inflammatory, memory health, antioxidant, heart health, mental health, anticancer properties

In the Fridge

- Dairy: Pasture-raised, grass-fed, organic butter, milk, and cheese (raw, if possible). Grass-fed and organic yogurt, sour cream, kefir, and cream. Low-pasteurized or

Teas and Coffee

Both tea and coffee can be sources of heavy metals, mold, mycotoxins, and pesticides. If consumed regularly, this may be an area to be more mindful of. I shop for organic teas and coffees because those are consumed daily in our home—sometimes multiple cups of tea a day. I also source brands that do third-party testing for other contaminants such as those I mentioned. Loose-leaf or tea crystals will ensure you're not inviting microplastics and other toxic materials into your body via tea bags. For tea in tea bags, avoid any in fancy shapes or that are shiny as those are typically higher in plastic content. Unbleached, paper tea bags are generally the less toxic option.

unpasteurized (from safe and healthy operations, of course), nonhomogenized, pasture-raised animals, A2 (a type of cow's milk that contains only A2 form of beta-casein protein and may be easier to digest for many).

- Fermented foods: Lacto-fermented pickles, sauerkraut, and kimchi. Kefir and plain yogurt. (We like the Greek style.)

- Eggs: If you've got your own chickens, awesome! If not, eggs from chickens raised outdoors are best. Look for pasture raised. If their supplement is organic, even better. (FYI: Chickens aren't vegetarian. So if the carton says "vegetarian fed," that's a red flag.)

- Meat: Like eggs, pasture raised is best. Grass-fed and grass-finished beef and lamb, pasture-raised pork and poultry.

A Word on "Natural" Flavor

Additional flavor compounds, contained in the vast majority of processed foods, are added to food products to produce smells and tastes, and to manipulate and enhance the taste of the end product. Flavor companies own the proprietary formulas of these concoctions, which may include upward of dozens to more than one hundred individual ingredients, all under the umbrella of "flavor"—whether artificial, natural, organic, or otherwise. "Natural" flavor may include ingredients such as BHA, BHT, diacetyl, and polysorbate 80. These "flavors" are trade secrets and protected, meaning finding out what the term *flavor* actually comprises in any given product is virtually impossible.

continued on page 24

How to Prepare Grains and Beans

Grains are really the seed of a plant. They are the part of the plant that contains all the information to grow more of that same plant, even years and years later. Because of this, they have numerous properties that help protect them from the environment so that they can survive and make new plants. It's their whole job.

All grains are seeds: This includes beans, legumes, rice, chia, lentils, nuts . . . all of them! The protective properties include things such as lectins and phytic acid and other constituents that, while keeping the seed protected, also make them difficult to break down—even by our human digestive systems. These compounds are often referred to as antinutrients as they make it difficult for our bodies to absorb, accrue, or process the nutrients the grain may contain.

Our ancestors had many ways of circumventing this obstacle. Traditionally prepared grains have the antinutrients decreased, making the grain easier on the body to digest and also making the resulting grain higher in absorbable nutrients. Soaking, sprouting, or fermenting grains can make the resulting food much more digestible and can greatly increase health benefits. A healthy gut is foundational to overall health and properly preparing grains like the traditional approach can be a great way to guard the gut. Properly prepared grains mean less gas and bloating: Less gut disruption means more nourishment.

How I Prepare Grains

I store dried organic grains such as beans in my pantry. At least one night before I plan on eating them, I will pour out a desired amount into a large glass bowl. I cover the grains with plenty of filtered water so that the grains are covered by 2 inches (5 cm) or more of water. I add a glug (about ¼ cup [60 ml]) of an acid. I typically use apple cider vinegar. Others sometimes use lemon juice or another acid. I cover with a clean towel or a loose lid to prevent dust or other unwanted things from landing in the bowl, and leave it on the counter eight hours or overnight. Then I drain the liquid out through a colander. I can then cook my grains however I wish.

For whole grains, it's worth leaving them to sprout for increased digestibility and greater health benefits. To sprout them: Place them in the colander (after soaking and draining) over a dish to catch any drips. Cover them loosely. You want air to be able to circulate but also keep out dust. Leave this in a cool, dark place, if possible. Mine is usually on my kitchen counter. In the morning and before bed, pour clean water over the grains still in the colander to rinse them and keep them damp. Return them to the sprouting place with the loose cover. Do this until sprouts appear. Then

eat, prepare, or cook however you like. Raw, sprouted lentils are great in a salad! Sprouted beans make the best chili that doesn't leave everyone stinking the place up.

Did you know canned beans are almost never soaked or sprouted, and they are almost always pressure-cooked in the very can you buy them in? The can itself is a toxic material and is typically lined with BPA, BPS, or other materials known to be toxic and problematic for our health. Heating the can to a high temperature to cook the contents makes leeching a higher likelihood, increasing the toxicity of the end product.

To make it easy to rely on homemade rather than store-bought, I prepare more than I need of a grain and store extra in wide-mouth canning jars in my freezer. (They can also be stored in silicone storage bags or other freezer-safe containers.) I just move a jar to the refrigerator overnight or the counter and later a bowl of warm water to plop them out and heat up.

This makes a great alternative to a can of beans. It is also a big-time money saver as dried beans and other grains are significantly less expensive than canned. Saves money. Less toxic. Better for your gut and health. Win, win, win.

23

- Artificial flavors: These are synthetic ingredients made in a lab designed to mimic the taste of natural ingredients or manipulate the taste of the end product. According to the U.S. Food and Drug Administration (FDA), artificial flavor is "any substance, the function of which is to impart flavor, which is not derived from a spice, fruit or fruit juice, vegetable or vegetable juice, edible yeast, herb, bark, bud, root, leaf or similar plant material, meat, fish, poultry, eggs, dairy products, or fermentation products thereof." These artificial flavors are often less expensive to produce and more stable from a chemical standpoint, which means they are advantageous to the manufacturer. The term is used to indicate proprietary chemicals owned by the flavor makers that create them. Their individual ingredients need not be fully disclosed to protect proprietary information as long as the ingredients used have been deemed GRAS ("generally regarded as safe") by the FDA.

- Natural flavors: These are almost the same as artificial flavors, but natural flavors are derived from substances found in nature, which may include animal parts, petroleum, wood pulp, and other materials we'd generally not choose to put in our food. They may also contain emulsifiers, preservatives, solvents, stabilizers, and other incidentals. Sometimes natural flavors may also be less sneaky ingredients such as vanillin or maple extract. Look for non-GMO natural flavors from companies you trust and get comfortable asking companies questions.

- Organic natural flavors: These are natural flavors that meet organic guidelines—at least 95 percent of the ingredients must be organic, with no synthetic solvents, carriers, or artificial preservatives. Organic natural flavors cannot contain additives such as benzoic acid, BHA, BHT, medium-chain triglycerides, mono- and diglycerides, polyglycerol esters of fatty acids, polysorbate 80, propylene glycol, or triacetin.

Stress Less, Cook More

Eating more food prepared at home, no matter the ingredients, is reported to drastically improve health outcomes. The goal here is making food with our own hands more often. Whether you're a seasoned cook who just needs some info on making things with better-for-you ingredients, or someone who is completely intimidated by cooking, I've got some tips to help make it simpler to be a healthier home cook.

Let go of extremes or perfectionism. The goal is to have less takeout, less highly processed foods, more home cookin'. This can be done without being the best cook. It can be done without following a diet to perfection. Just make more food yourself. Watch it become easier and even more fun over time. See how it can improve your health, your mood, your energy, your sleep, and more.

A little prep makes a huge difference. If you can, chop, measure out, and set aside ingredients before dinner prep time. This might be the night before, during kids' naptime, or at a time that makes sense for you. It will save you some time during dinner prep later.

Mise en place is French for "put in place" or "gather." Set up your work station with all you might need at hand and organized. This should include cutting board(s), tools, ingredients, and a garbage or scrap bowl.

A sharp knife is a safer knife. You don't need the world's best knife to chop well—a sharp knife helps, though! And it can prevent injury, unlike many may think. A dull knife requires more pressure; this increases incidences of slipping and unintentional cuts that lead to injury. A sharp knife requires less force, which keeps you in more control of the knife, and can lower incidence of injury. I have very inexpensive knives currently that have served me well for more than a decade with a little personal knife sharpener I keep in a kitchen drawer. One day I'll have some fancier knives, and I'll get those professionally sharpened a couple times a year. Some home-use sharpeners can be helpful. There are also professional knife-sharpening services offered at some farmers' markets, home goods stores, and mail-away services as well.

No meal plans necessary. In different seasons of life, this prep concept can take on different appearances. When I had two little ones under the age of two, a meal game plan for the next day meant chopping and measuring at night once everyone was asleep for their longest stretch. I'd either put everything into a casserole dish at night to throw in the oven the next evening or toss most everything into a slow cooker in the morning. Now that I have a little more flexibility and my kids aren't quite as fully dependent on me, just before bedtime I take a look at what we have on hand and decide what we'll have the next evening. I'll also move a protein from the freezer to the refrigerator and soak any grains needed overnight.

Keep staples stocked. Having a pantry and freezer stocked with some common staples helps me to throw together a meal using whatever fresh ingredients I have on hand. This can take some practice, but knowing I can grab a cup or two of broth and some frozen vegetables from my freezer, pasta or rice from the pantry, and whatever meat and fresh produce I have helps me to prepare a nourishing meal for my family without fuss.

Another safety tip for cutting and chopping:

Add a damp paper towel under your cutting board to help hold it steady as you use it. This helps to prevent the board from moving and lowers the risk of cutting yourself. Use the paper towel afterward to help wipe the counter.

Clean as you go. My mama taught me this, and I teach it to my kids too. No one wants to have to clean up a kitchen disaster after laboring to create a meal and sitting down to enjoy it! Any inactive time during cooking, such as waiting for water to come to a boil or the oven to preheat, is a good time to clean a few things up. I use that time to wash dishes and put away things I've finished using. My goal is to always leave as little mess as possible by the time the meal is served so I can sit down and enjoy the meal and not dread any aftermath. This also enables me to spend more time with those I served after the meal has ended as cleanup takes such little time, usually.

Get comfortable with seasoning. This doesn't need to be complicated. Properly seasoning with salt alone can make a world of difference, and many people simply just do not know what that looks like. Just as a side

note, I remember watching cooking shows with friends and hearing "That's a lot of salt!" often. I got to wondering, "Is it, really?" If you look at how much salt or sodium is in your premade or packaged foods, what chefs and good home cooks use in the kitchen pales in comparison!

Get comfortable using salt and know that home-cooked meals are virtually always going to have much, much less sodium than restaurant and packaged foods. In addition to salt, there are so many wonderful seasonings to incorporate to really elevate your cooking. I used to use a blend of "everyday seasonings" and finally took a look at what was actually in it. It had some great spices, many of which I already had in my cupboard. Most spice and seasoning blends also have added sugars, anticaking agents, and preservatives I don't need or want in my food. I bought some of those "everyday" spices individually (e.g., coriander, paprika, garlic, onion, and mustard) and started using those more in my cooking. Seasoning well can really take your meals to another level.

Taste as you go. Every tomato, carrot, or bunch of parsley, even from the same garden, can have different pungency and flavors. If a recipe calls for a certain amount of seasoning, you might need a little more or less than the recipe creator lists, and they know this too. A good cook learns to taste the dish along the way and adjust seasonings to

make the final dish as flavorful and balanced as possible. When making a dish, even following the most tried-and-true recipe, it's important to taste the dish along the way. In my kitchen, we all know my saying, "Taste and see . . . that the Lord is good, and adjust your seasonings as needed."

Building a nourishing plate. You can get very scientific with this, and I think there is a time and place for that. I want to encourage you to not overthink this unless truly necessary. I focus on protein and fiber and color, and I find that that is essentially the foundation of a very nourishing meal. Protein and fiber carry with them myriad health benefits and implications. When you have quality protein and plenty of fiber, I find that you often have most, if not all, of the other important stuff too, as it comes with the territory.

Put plenty of good-quality protein and high-fiber foods on your plate, and make sure there's some color on it, and you'll find yourself a nourishing meal. High-quality protein is going to bring with it some healthy fats, bioavailable vitamins and minerals, amino acids, and more. High-protein foods include beef, poultry, fish, eggs, dairy, garbanzo beans, nuts, and seeds. Foods naturally rich in fiber (e.g., apples, sweet potato, berries, quinoa, legumes) bring essential vitamins, minerals, and antioxidant. Protein and fiber are slower digesting. They help you feel satiated and nourished longer, while also helping reduce blood sugar spikes and prevent energy crashes, and they help your body to remain in better balance. Protein helps to satiate, regulate blood sugar, and balance your meal and your body, and it is energizing. Colorful foods contain beneficial compounds and components such as antioxidants, polyphenols, and a wide variety of important vitamins and minerals.

The power of presentation. When a meal looks appetizing, it truly can taste better. Don't overcomplicate this, but don't ignore this very simple practice. It can make a huge impact on how much you and those you serve can appreciate and enjoy their meal. A meal well enjoyed can be better digested, and that has its own health benefits too. I love a plain white plate or shallow bowl to really showcase my food.

Consider how the food will look when it's plated or combined. If you can make this look a little prettier, do it! For example, with a stew-type meal that can otherwise look like mush, I love to plate this in a shallow bowl. I'll add the scoop of rice or quinoa like a beautiful island in the middle. Sprinkle on a pop of color with some microgreens or minced cilantro or parsley. Sprinkle some flaky salt, or a pinch of paprika for a pop of color. Separate beige items with something colorful. Serve a yogurt parfait in a pretty glass. Be a little more thoughtful and get creative! For me

it's kind of like the difference between handing someone a gift, unwrapped and stuffed in a plastic bag, and a gift that has been thoughtfully wrapped in crisp paper, with a handwritten tag and beautiful bow. It just feels more special. Make each meal be received as the beautiful gift that it truly is.

My Shopping (and Money-Saving) Tips

We often hear people recommend that we shop the outside edges of the grocery store. The reason is that this is where we find the majority of whole foods (e.g., fresh fruits and vegetables, raw meats, eggs, and dairy). The closer we get to the center of most grocery stores, the more concentrated the aisles are with packaged foods, most of which are highly processed and contain many ingredients that aren't so whole or nourishing.

I love this concept, and I want to encourage you to take it a bit further: Build the base of your grocery list with whole, fresh foods. In-season fruits and vegetables are a goal. For the items you can't get whole and fresh and in season, explore the frozen section for options. Many times there are excellent options there for fruits, vegetables, and even meats that can provide high-quality ingredients and oftentimes at a lower cost. Some frozen items are even fresher than the unfrozen goods. For example, a large percentage of

refrigerated meat at the grocery store, including fish, was previously frozen. By purchasing it thawed, you may be getting meat that is already less fresh than those still frozen. Again, many times, the frozen options are lower cost!

When purchasing foods that require any amount of processing, aim for those that required less manufacturing. For example, oils that are often touted as healthy in one way or another by the food industry are oftentimes very highly processed, using solvents, deodorizers, bleaching agents, and more to turn something like canola into a clear and mostly odorless oil. Opt for those with less processing and time-honored health benefits such as cold-pressed olive oil, unrefined coconut oil, and traditional cooking fats such as pure butter and duck fat.

For other packaged foods, look for those with ingredients you would use in your own home and can find in your own pantry. This is not always easy. The good news is that packaged foods are more costly than whole foods. Someone has to incur the cost for all that labor and manufacturing. When we buy less highly processed foods and packaged goods, we can save money.

When to Buy Organic

My personal priorities for buying organic when possible include items that are more heavily treated with pesticides and herbicides, antibiotics, steroids, and hormones, or have unsanitary and inhumane living conditions. This includes dairy products; meat, poultry, and seafood; eggs; and most grains, nuts, and seeds.

For produce I appreciate tools such as the Dirty Dozen and Clean 15 produced by the Environmental Working Group (EWG) every year listing produce items with the highest and lowest levels of pesticides that year. If buying all organic produce is not an option, aim for buying organic from the Dirty Dozen list. In addition to this, genetically modified crops (GMOs) are often modified to be able to withstand higher amounts of pesticides than before their modifications. For this reason, I prefer to buy organic when the particular produce item has a GMO version.

I also try to buy organic when it comes to processed or packaged goods. These items, such as bars, crackers, chips, boxed or canned soups, milks, broths, and other snacks, can have a wide variety of ingredients that I prefer to avoid hiding in the ingredients list, such as GMOs, high amounts of sugars, artificial sweeteners, MSG, inflammatory oils, gums, dyes, and preservatives. Buying these items organic means they will not have artificial dyes, sweeteners, preservatives, or flavorings; GMOs; added hormones; glyphosate or other inorganic pesticides or chemicals; antibiotics; high-fructose corn syrup; hydrogenated oils; or BHT/BHA.

10 Budget-Friendly Food Tips for A Little Less Toxic Kitchen

1. Buy fewer packaged food items. Whole foods typically cost less than packaged foods, and they can be stretched much further.

2. Buy more in season. Fruit or vegetables grown across the world are going to cost more because they have to be shipped to get to your store.

3. Use tools such as the EWG Dirty Dozen to help determine which food items you buy organically, if buying all organic is not in the budget.

4. Use frozen whole foods. Try frozen berries for smoothies or frozen vegetables for roasting and adding to soups, stews, and casseroles.

5. Buy some items in bulk to save money. I often shop bulk bins or retailers that sell in bulk for items that have a long shelf life, such as beans, rice, quinoa, lentils, popcorn, peas, salt, certain spices, and sweeteners.

6. Shop around. Online apps and sites make it easy to compare prices and find sales. Wait for sales and stock up. Some online markets have prices that consistently match or beat local shops.

7. Make use of that freezer! When I find good-quality meat on sale, I stock up and load up my freezer. Stored properly, meats can be kept frozen safely for months.

8. Eat out less. Eating out is almost always much more expensive than preparing food at home. Even once or twice less a month makes a big difference in the budget. Allocate those savings to better-quality food or other needs in the home.

9. Eat more plants. Meat can be a very nourishing part of a balanced diet. Eating meat at every meal may not be the most sustainable way to eat well on a budget. We prioritize buying quality meat over quantity and eat meat fewer times a day or fewer times a week.

10. Read the ingredients before adding items to your cart. Make a conscious choice to read what you're inviting into your home. You will be less likely to add items with fun labels and convenience foods that cost more but aren't as filling or nourishing.

Cooking and Eating with Kids

"How do you get your kids to eat so healthy?" This is one of the most common comments or questions I get. I understand. I have spent a large portion of my life working with children, from my babysitting days, to my classroom-teaching days, to raising my own children and being around many children in similar age ranges to my own regularly. Although I have a lot of experience and training, I don't consider myself the end-all child expert. However, here is what

helped me approach this with my kids in a way that is working well . . . so far! Time will tell, but I do hope I have helped to lay a great foundation here that they will return to when they're grown.

- **I don't "get" my kids to eat anything.** I make choices for them as their parent on many things, because they're incapable of making some of those choices themselves yet. I choose what we eat and when. They choose *if* they will eat it and how much they will eat. No pressure. No bribing, begging, or manipulation. They have control over the situation, and that is empowering to them. If there is

a whiff of pressure or manipulation or fear, kids pick up on that and they most often will respond with resistance. Who wants to feel controlled or pressured about food?! Not me. Not them.

- **Create a pressure-free zone.** I serve what I believe to be nourishing for our bodies with what I'm able, and I try to make it look pretty, taste yummy, and be a happy experience. I serve the food. If there's an objection, then this is what the kids hear from me: "Eat what you like. Leave what you don't." That's it. No drama. Our table is a pressure-free zone and a place to connect, discover, learn, and just be.

- **I model expectations around food.**
As I've mentioned, I truly view food as fuel and so much more. My kids see my personal relationship with food, and I believe we are their greatest role models in all things—and this matters. I don't barter or bribe. Food isn't a negotiating tool. It is our fuel, and we have the ability to make that fuel fun and delicious, and to be creative with it. We can make things to our particular tastes and preferences, and we can do so while meeting our nutritional needs.

- **Involve them.** My kids have both sat beside my cutting board on the counter since they were old enough to do so. As early as one year old or even earlier they would help me add ingredients, watch me chop, help me mix, scoop, and stir. When they got old enough, I got them kid-safe knives and gave them jobs they could manage with minimal intervention. They enjoy being included, and they appreciate the control they have when they help create as the choppers, mashers, and mixers. Being a part of the process helps them to have appreciation for the food they're being served. It helps them know their taste and opinion is valued. It helps them feel like they are a part of fueling the family team that we are!

- **Do not break trust.** I don't hide or sneak ingredients. I never want my kids to fear there might be something unexpected in their meal.

I want them to trust me and to know what they are eating. Break that trust and watch them resist and restrict foods more. I don't manipulate. I don't beg. I don't barter. This is how we fuel in our home, and we make it yummy and fun.

- **I try to educate, empower, and equip them.** I am doing my best to educate my kids about their bodies and how important food is for their health. I do not want to instill fear. I take this approach so that they might continue to love many foods and learn how to keep their bodies strong with what we have been so blessed to fuel them with. And so they have a good foundation to return to as they grow. We talk about what a protein is and where we can get fiber. We talk about healthy fats, vitamins, minerals, and beneficial bacteria.

- **I don't restrict. I take responsibility.** Let me elaborate. We all may have different interpretations of what *restrict* means when it comes to food. I certainly will not allow my children to run into a street, leave with strange adults, or stay up until they decide it's bedtime. I am their parent, and it is my responsibility to make decisions for their health and safety and to teach them how to make good decisions for themselves until they are old enough and capable of doing that on their own. I must do the same with food. I wouldn't let them eat so many cookies they get sick.

I also don't want to have them eating things I know are undermining their health and leading to future pain and suffering. If we are at a party and the food offered is not what I would serve at home, we eat it, with gratitude, provided it's not something that will make us have a bad reaction. (For us, that's currently gluten and dye.) One day they'll be making their own choices about food full-time, and my hope is that I will have equipped them with a healthy foundation they can return to.

It's Not Too Late to Start

If your children are older and you're just starting out, or if a child is limited or restrictive on what they will eat or hesitant to try different foods, you can still help them. Start with the tips I've already listed. If you need additional resources, see the Resources section (page 200).

- Start very slowly. Do not make huge changes all at once.

- Make the things they already love and start doing that with better-for-them ingredients and with your own hands.

- Little by little, small and pressure-free exposures over time can help. Exposure can contribute to decreased aversion and increased curiosity.

- Don't serve a full plate of a nonpreferred food item or meal and expect your child (or anyone!) to go for that. I wouldn't put a plate

covered in melted cheese in front of my child who is currently "on a break" from melted cheese (aka hates the very sight of it) and get frustrated the child doesn't eat anything. I will serve my family the same meal and reserve a portion without cheese for that child. I can make accommodations without becoming a short-order cook.

About My Recipes

There are many diets out there. The *A Little Less Toxic* approach to food is not a diet. I think of it as a way of life. It doesn't have a rigid set of rules or universal guidelines like some diets do (e.g., carnivore, or Paleo, or vegan). Eating the *A Little Less Toxic* way can be for anyone. My philosophy for food and everything else is: "Do what you can, with what you're able, and as it makes sense for you." My goal is that even if you subscribe to a special diet, you can still be A Little Less Toxic as well.

Here's an overview of what you'll find in my food philosophy and in my recipes.

Restrictions, Special Diets, and Gluten

I don't encourage removing entire food groups (outside of health reasons, such as allergies or true sensitivities, or for temporary seasons for testing or healing). That said, I have had to learn what my body reacts to and take that into consideration. This can change over time for each person as they bring healing to their guts and get their bodies into better balance.

For all of my recipes, I hope that you can make modifications to meet your unique needs. For example, I am currently not dairy-free, but I was dairy-free for a long time and made most of these recipes without dairy during those years by either omitting the dairy or utilizing a substitute nondairy milk or cheese. Likewise, meat in most of my recipes can be swapped for things such as sprouted lentils, beans, or other vegetarian proteins.

One thing you'll notice though is that all of my recipes are gluten-free. I have been gluten-free since 2013, when I tested numerous foods to see if I reacted to them. Personally, I have learned through trial and error over the years that I am able to maintain better health without gluten. That remains true to this day (with notable exceptions, such as if it is properly fermented in something like a sourdough). Thus, I have found ways to make all of my favorite things without gluten, and that's what you'll find in my recipes. If you do well with gluten, by all means use your favorite pastas and flours with gluten in place of mine! I just can't tell you what works best for things such as flours with gluten because I cannot test and taste them.

Ingredients and Sourcing

It probably comes as no surprise, but when it comes to ingredients, I recommend turning packages around and looking at the ingredients lists before purchasing. Marketing claims and health claims can be convincing, but they are not the full story. It's what's inside that counts. Aim for more whole-food ingredients. When in doubt, try making it yourself.

Meat: Ideally, meat should be pasture-raised, grass-fed or grass-finished, wild-caught, and local.

Dairy: I like raw, organic, from animals raised on pasture and locally.

Produce: I try to find as much as I can that is organic and local, especially those on the annual update of the EWG's Dirty Dozen list.

Grains: I recommend organic and traditionally prepared for digestibility (meaning fermented or soaked or sprouted; see page 20). Long and slow cooking or pressure cooking for things such as beans, after soaking or sprouting, is ideal. Heirloom varieties such as einkorn, spelt, and Kamut are great options.

Packaged foods: Everyone buys packaged foods to some extent. My rule of thumb is to buy things with ingredients I'd use at home if I were making it myself. The less processed, the better. I also avoid oils that are highly processed and can be more inflammatory than others, especially with consistent exposure. I prefer unrefined sweeteners such as honey, maple syrup, coconut sugar, and dates. Things such as pasta noodles should have one to two ingredients.

Use the ALLT Approach to Make Mealtime **A L**ittle **L**ess **T**oxic!

A Assess: Take inventory and consider what items are actually used and needed. If it's been sitting in a drawer or the back of the pantry for over a year, it's not only probably not needed, but likely expired. Keep only things you really need. Note: Once you get better at this, I can almost promise this list will become even shorter over time.

L Let go: If it's expired or unnecessary and contributing to clutter or toxic burden, find it a new home. That may very well be the garbage, unfortunately.

L Level up: As an item runs low or needs to be replaced, look for an alternative with healthier ingredients. Do not wait until you're at empty: You'll most likely grab the same old thing or something with compelling marketing on the label at the local drugstore.

T Transform over time: As soon as you get rid of one item or replace it with something healthier, your space is immediately less toxic! Over time this will multiply and compound—watch how quickly small things add up.

Chapter 2

Nourishing Breakfasts

DIY Açai Bowl with Rich Maple Granola

We have a lot of local shops that sell these bowls, but they tend to be quite expensive . . . and full of sugar. Because we love eating them, I started working with the unsweetened açai packets. Top these with whatever you have on hand: fresh fruit, shredded coconut, honey, bee pollen. But pretty much any time I make these I make the granola too. Greek yogurt adds a good amount of protein and takes it another step away from being an unfilling sugar bomb. When it comes to the frozen fruit, I like blueberries, raspberries, or mixed berries. Pineapple or mango would also be delicious.

Yield: Serves 4

Ingredients:

½ cup (118 ml) water (Milk or orange juice also work.)

2 packages (3½ ounces, or 198 g) frozen unsweetened açai berries

1 cup (236 g) frozen fruit of choice

2 frozen bananas

1 cup (240 g) plain full-fat Greek yogurt

Rich Maple Granola (recipe follows)

Other Topping Ideas:

Sliced banana, berries, sliced kiwi, hemp hearts, bee pollen, raw honey, sprouted sunflower or pumpkin seeds, shredded coconut

1. In a blender, add the water, açai berries, fruit, and yogurt. Blend up until smooth. Use the tamper in your blender if you have one. It helps to move things around to blend everything thoroughly.

2. Pour into four bowls and add a spoonful or two of granola to each. Add any toppings you like.

Tip: *Adding the liquid to the bottom of your blender first makes it easier to blend together.*

The Power of Açai Berries

Açai berries are native to Brazil. They are high in antioxidants, resume production of free radicals, and:

• Are high in fiber

• Are low glycemic

• Are rich in an array of vitamins and minerals

• Are yummy

Rich Maple Granola

Favorite batch of granola yet. So good. Good for you. No refined sugars. Loaded with protein and iron and minerals galore. Made a TON. And I'm not mad about it.

Yield: Makes about 6 cups

Ingredients:

4 cups (400 g) gluten-free rolled oats

1 cup (150 g) nuts or seeds, sprouted if you have them (I added sprouted pumpkin and sunflower seeds.)

2 tablespoons (16 g) freshly ground flax seeds

2 tablespoons (20 g) hemp hearts

1 tablespoon (8 g) ground cinnamon

¼ teaspoon sea salt

3 tablespoons (27 g) coconut sugar (optional)

¼ cup (59 ml) coconut oil, melted

¼ cup (59 ml) raw honey

3 tablespoons (44 ml) maple syrup

2 tablespoons (30 ml) molasses

1 teaspoon vanilla extract

1 large egg white

1. Preheat the oven to 350°F (175°C). Line a baking sheet with parchment paper.

2. In a large bowl, mix together the oats, nuts, seeds, hemp hearts, cinnamon, salt, and coconut sugar, if using.

3. In another bowl, combine the melted coconut oil, honey, maple syrup, molasses, and vanilla. Pour this over the dry ingredients, and mix to combine.

4. In a small bowl or cup, whisk the egg white until frothy. Stir that into the mixture.

5. Spread the granola on the lined baking sheet. Bake for 15 to 20 minutes until crispy and golden. Be careful not to let it burn.

6. Remove the granola from the oven and let cool. Break it up using your hands.

How to Store: *Store in an airtight container for up to 2 weeks. You can also freeze the extra if you don't gobble it all up immediately.*

Cast-Iron Dutch Baby Pancake with Warm Berry Compote

Dutch babies may look fancy (and even sound sort of fancy!), but they are easy to make and easy to scale. Once a year, my family goes on a big old extended family trip to Temecula, California. We're talking at least twenty people to feed for every meal, so we rotate who cooks. But after the last few years, I now *have to* volunteer for breakfast because this recipe is in high demand. Even the pickiest of eaters love it.

While I love doing these in a cast-iron skillet, you can totally make them in a glass baking dish. For toppings, you can just go with good-quality maple syrup, but they do shine with the fruit and powdered sugar. And the berry compote doesn't add much time or effort, but does add a wonderful extra layer of flavor.

Yield: Serves 4

Ingredients:

5 tablespoons (69 g) salted butter

6 large eggs

1 cup (237 ml) milk
(Any type will work.)

1 teaspoon vanilla extract

Pinch of sea salt

1 cup (120 g) gluten-free flour
(I used Bob's Red Mill 1:1
gluten-free blend.)

Optional:

Powdered sugar and
fresh strawberries, sliced

Warm Berry Compote
(recipe follows)

1. Preheat the oven to 400°F (200°C).

2. Add the butter to a 10-inch (25-cm) cast-iron skillet or other oven-safe pan (such as an 8 × 8-inch [20 × 20-cm] baking dish). Place the skillet in the oven while you prepare the batter. Keep your eye on it and remove it when the butter has melted.

Note: *You can also let the butter brown a little bit, which tastes really good. Just don't let it burn.*

3. In a large bowl, whisk together the eggs, milk, vanilla, and salt. Sift or simply add the flour, whisking until there are no lumps.

4. At this point, your pan should be out of the oven (or nearly there). Carefully pour the batter into the hot pan full of melted butter. Place an oven mitt or dish towel over the handle to remind yourself the pan is hot.

continued on following page

5. Transfer back to the oven and bake for 15 minutes until puffed up and slightly golden.

6. Remove from the oven, and top with powdered sugar and fresh strawberries if desired.

7. Slice and serve while still warm, offering warm berry compote on the side.

Tip: *You can make powdered coconut sugar by blending coconut sugar and a bit of tapioca flour until you get the powdery texture you want.*

Warm Berry Compote

Yield: Serves 6 to 8

Ingredients:

2 cups (473 ml) fresh or frozen berries of choice (I use a frozen mixed berry blend.)

2 tablespoons (30 ml) maple syrup or raw honey, or to taste

Zest and juice of 1 small lemon

Pinch of sea salt

1. In a small saucepan, heat the berries over medium-low heat. Maintain a simmer, stirring occasionally, until they are soft and the liquid has reduced by about a third.

2. Add the remaining ingredients, and stir to combine.

3. Serve while still warm alongside the Dutch baby pancake.

How to Store: *Extra compote can be cooled and stored in an airtight container in the refrigerator for up to 2 weeks.*

French Toast Casserole

This is a recipe where it's best to make it the night before, cover, and store in the refrigerator to bake the next morning. That means no more preservative-laden cinnamon rolls or other pop-open-and-enjoy baked goods are needed come Christmas morning! As an added bonus, the cinnamon makes the house smell amazing as you snuggle around the fire, peek in stockings, and exchange gifts.

The directions are pretty foolproof as written. It has a traditional French toast texture where it's custardy and spongy, and the top has a nice crunch. I've found tart berries add a good balance to the sweetness and all that maple syrup. Go ahead and pop some bacon or sausage in the oven at the same time. A delicious breakfast will be waiting for you when you're ready.

Yield: Serves 4

Ingredients:

1 loaf of your favorite bread, such as white, multigrain, or cinnamon raisin

8–10 large eggs

1 teaspoon vanilla extract

Pinch of sea salt

½ teaspoon ground cinnamon

¼–½ cup (59–118 ml) maple syrup

Splash of milk (Any type will work.)

1–1½ cups (150–225 g) fresh or frozen berries

3–4 tablespoons (42–55 g) salted butter, cut into small pieces and divided

For Serving:

Powdered sugar

1. Line an 8 × 8-inch (20 × 20-cm) casserole dish or rimmed pan with parchment paper. Alternately, you can grease it with butter.

2. Cut the loaf of bread into 1-inch (2.5-cm) cubes. Transfer the cubed bread to the casserole dish.

3. In a large bowl or large measuring cup, whisk the eggs with the vanilla, salt, cinnamon, maple syrup, and milk.

4. Pour the egg mixture over the bread. Give it a little stir to combine. Don't overdo it to where the cubes start to break down, but even out the moisture as best you can.

5. Top with the fresh or frozen berries, and dot evenly with about 2 tablespoons (28 g) of butter.

6. Cover the dish with a piece of parchment paper and then aluminum foil. Pop in the fridge for at least 30 minutes but preferably overnight.

7. When you're ready to bake, place the covered dish in a preheated 350°F (175°C) oven and bake for 30 minutes. Remove the cover and bake for 15 minutes, or until the top is toasted and golden brown.

8. Top with the remaining pieces of butter and dust with powdered sugar. Serve warm.

Grain-Free Chocolate Chip Banana Bread

As soon as I have a few bananas going bad, it's time for this bread. I worked on this recipe while I was on my gluten-free journey. It's a fairly classic banana bread recipe with a little crisp on the top and a nice, soft middle. It's fluffy and moist. This recipe also works well if you want to make it in muffin tins.

Yield: Makes one 8½ × 4½ × 2½-inch (22 × 11 × 6-cm) loaf

Ingredients:

4 large eggs

4 very ripe bananas

¼ cup (57 g) butter, ghee, or vegan butter of choice, melted

½ cup (125 g) peanut butter or nut butter of choice (Use sun butter for a nut-free option.)

½ cup (62 g) coconut flour

1 teaspoon baking soda

1 teaspoon baking powder

1 teaspoon vanilla extract

Generous pinch of sea salt

½–1 cup (100–170 g) semisweet chocolate chips

Optional, for Serving:

Butter

1. Preheat the oven to 350°F (175°C). Line an 8½ × 4½ × 2½-inch (22 × 11 × 6-cm) loaf pan with parchment paper, or grease it with butter or coconut oil.

2. In a blender or food processor, add everything but the chocolate chips. Mix until combined. Alternatively, whisk the eggs and mash the bananas by hand before stirring in the rest.

3. Stir in the chocolate chips.

4. Pour the batter into the loaf pan. Bake for 45 minutes until a toothpick comes out clean.

5. Serve sliced with butter, if desired, and enjoy.

Tips: *You can use this batter to make muffins. Fill a muffin tin with liners and add the batter to reach about two-thirds of the way full. Bake at 400°F (200°C) for 25 to 30 minutes until a toothpick comes out clean.*

Before adding the liners, scatter a pinch of uncooked rice in the bottom of each pocket to keep the bottoms drier.

Next-Day Oatmeal Muffins

One day at my house a switch flipped: My kids went from big oatmeal eaters to just not touching it. Now, it goes back and forth. So any time they snub my oatmeal, it becomes the base for these muffins for the next day, which they never turn down. These get a nice crust on top with a fluffy inside. Experiment with mix-ins—I like peaches, other berries, and dried cranberries.

Yield: Makes 12 muffins

Ingredients:

1 tablespoon (15 ml) coconut oil

2 cups (100 g) cooked oats (see note)

1½ cups (144 g) blanched almond flour

½ cup (118 ml) maple syrup

1 teaspoon baking powder

1 teaspoon vanilla extract or powder

2 large eggs

Pinch of sea salt

1 teaspoon ground cinnamon

¾–1 cup (130–175 g) sliced or chopped fruit

Optional: pinch of coconut sugar for sprinkling

1. Preheat the oven to 400°F (200°C). Line a 12-cup muffin tin with parchment paper liners.

Tip: *Scatter a bit of rice under the muffin tin liners to keep the bottoms drier.*

2. In a large bowl, combine all the ingredients. Stir gently to mix.

3. Scoop the batter into the muffin tin, filling each cup about two-thirds of the way.

4. Sprinkle the tops with coconut sugar if you're feeling fancy.

5. Bake for 25 to 30 minutes until a toothpick comes out clean.

Note: *If you don't have leftover cooked oats, simply mix 1½ cups (150 g) of rolled oats with 1½ cups (355 ml) of water in a 2-quart (1.9-L) saucepan. Bring to a boil, reduce to a simmer, and cover. Cook for about 12 minutes.*

Pressure-Cooked Eggs with Hash Browns and Oven Bacon

There are countless tips and tricks for boiling eggs perfectly, and I'm sure a lot of them are really good, but I've gotten the best results by using the electric pressure cooker. I can make a large batch as well—a couple dozen in my large pressure cooker. But eggs on their own do not make a complete breakfast. Enter the hash browns: Most from the store have inflammatory oils and preservatives, so the convenience option was out. Fortunately, I found making them at home is super easy and I've never looked back. Last but not least, oven-baked bacon turns out perfect, and it goes well with cooking the eggs in the pressure cooker for a low-mess breakfast.

Yield: Serves 4+

Note: *This is to serve 4–6 people. You can cook more or fewer eggs without changing the instructions.*

Ingredients:
1 cup (237 ml) water
8–12 large eggs
Hash Browns (recipe follows)
Oven Bacon (recipe follows)

1. In the Instant Pot, add the water and the included rack insert. Add as many eggs as you want to make.

2. Set the pressure to high for 3 minutes for soft-boiled, 4 minutes for medium-boiled, and 5 minutes for hard-boiled.

3. Meanwhile, fill a bowl with ice water while the eggs cook.

4. As soon as the time is up, release the pressure manually. Using tongs, carefully take out the eggs and place them in the ice water bath for 5 minutes.

5. Remove the eggs from the ice water, peel, and serve with hash browns and bacon.

Tip: *Don't skip the ice water bath! It stops the eggs from cooking, resulting in perfectly cooked eggs. And it makes them easier to peel! These eggs can be stored in the refrigerator for up to 1 week.*

Hash Browns

We've been on a serious hash brown kick. If you don't have an Instant Pot, you can poke and bake the potatoes at 350°F (175°C) for about 30 minutes, then use them or store them in the refrigerator for up to a few days before shredding and cooking. Refrigerating cooked potatoes before use can make these even healthier as they can greatly increase their resistant starch and lower their glycemic impact. Resistant starch is fuel for healthy gut microbes, and a healthy gut microbiome is a major key to a healthier you.

Yield: Serves 4 to 6

Ingredients:

3–4 medium russet potatoes

2 tablespoons (30 ml) fat of
choice (I like duck fat when
I can get some.)

Sea salt, to taste

Tip: *Don't overthink this. We're just frying up potatoes here. One big thing is to not mess with them—let them sit in the hot pan and get good and crispy before flipping.*

1. Heat up a cast-iron or wide-bottom stainless steel pan over medium heat.

2. Shred the potatoes. Add the fat to the hot pan.

3. Add about 1 cup (85 g) or a big handful of the shredded spuds at a time. Flatten a little with your hand or a spatula.

4. Season with salt. Cook undisturbed for about 5 minutes until the potato pile slides around easily. Flip carefully and cook on the other side for 3 to 5 minutes until crispy. Add a little more fat in between flipping if needed.

5. Serve hot.

Oven Bacon

Ingredients:

As many bacon slices as you need

1. Line a baking sheet with parchment paper, and line a dish with a paper towel. Lay the slices of bacon on the parchment paper, and place the baking sheet in a cool oven. Set the oven to 400°F (200°C) and cook for 18 to 20 minutes until crispy, checking toward the end of cooking time.

2. Move the perfectly cooked bacon to the lined dish until ready to serve. Save the bacon grease for cooking something else!

Family-Style Breakfast Tacos

These came about because my kids were burned-out on breakfast options, but they always want lunch and dinner foods. So, I took one of their later-in-the-day favorites and brought it to the breakfast table. These days I serve this family style for a build-your-own-taco experience, and it's a huge hit. You can switch up the fillings as much as you want—and, in fact, I suspect it's why kids love it when you make these.

Yield: Serves 4

Ingredients:

1 pound (454 g) ground breakfast sausage, pork, beef, or turkey

Optional: ½–1 teaspoon taco seasoning (If the meat is unseasoned; see page 148 for recipe.)

Sea salt, to taste

8 large eggs

6–12 tortillas, warmed (We do small street taco–size shells for these, which is in the 10–12 shells range.)

2 cups (342 g) cooked pinto or black beans, or 1 can (15½ ounces, or 439 g), drained and rinsed

Optional Toppings:

Guacamole or sliced avocado

Shredded cabbage

Shredded raw Cheddar cheese

Finely chopped fresh cilantro

Salsa

Hot sauce

1. In a 10-inch (25-cm) skillet, cook the meat for 7 to 10 minutes until brown, stirring occasionally. Add the taco seasoning and salt to taste toward the end of cooking time.

2. In a large skillet, cook the eggs however you prefer. (We like scrambled or eggs over medium.)

3. In serving dishes, put out the warm tortillas along with the cooked eggs and beans, as well as any other taco fillings your family enjoys. Let everyone create their own breakfast taco.

Crispy Potato and Egg Bake

This is a casserole I make for people when they need a little comfort, whether they just had a baby or are going through a hard time. I have found over the years that even when everyone is dropping off food, this one is appreciated because it's rare to get a breakfast dish in those situations. Note that you can swap out the potatoes for Tater Tots: It's just a struggle to find tots with good ingredients. And don't worry; the real potatoes melt right in but still get a nice crunch on top (unlike many traditional recipes that have potatoes only on the bottom).

Yield: Serves 4 to 6

Ingredients:

2 tablespoons (28 g) salted butter

4 medium russet potatoes, cooked (see note)

2 tablespoons (30 ml) avocado oil, extra-virgin olive oil, beef tallow, or duck fat

1½ teaspoons sea salt, divided

12 large eggs

½ large red bell pepper, diced (about ½ cup [90 g])

½ cup (115 g) chopped fresh or frozen spinach

1¼ cups (104 g) shredded cheese of choice, divided

Optional:

1 cup (454 g) chopped cooked breakfast meat, such as bacon, sausage, and ham

¼ teaspoon black pepper

1. Preheat the oven to 350°F (175°C). Grease an 8 × 8-inch (20 × 20-cm) baking dish with the butter.

2. Shred the cooked potatoes and place them in a large bowl. You should have about 4 cups (624 g). Toss with the oil and 1 teaspoon of the salt.

3. In another large bowl, whisk the eggs. Stir in the bell pepper, spinach, 1 cup (83 g) of the cheese, meat (if using), and the remaining salt and the pepper. Mix until everything is incorporated well. Pour into the greased dish.

4. Top the egg mixture with the remaining cheese to help make a "shelf" of sorts for the potatoes. Top with the shredded potatoes.

5. Bake for 1 hour to 1 hour and 15 minutes until the top is golden brown and crispy and the eggs are cooked through. You can pop it in the broiler for 2 to 4 minutes, keeping a close watch, to crisp it up a bit more if needed.

6. Let sit for 5 minutes before serving.

Note: *You can either pressure-cook the potatoes for 4 minutes or bake them at 350°F (175°C) for 30 to 40 minutes.*

Build Your Own Yogurt Bowl

This looks beautiful but is one of the easiest breakfasts. It's a lot like the DIY Açai Bowl (page 40), if your family is into the choose-your-own-adventure bowl type of breakfast. I like to load these up with all sorts of protein, omega-3s, and healthy fats. I just try to go for clean and simple ingredients and plain yogurt (or coconut yogurt) without any added sugar. Experiment with jams, honey, maple syrup, or whatever you'd like to sweeten to taste.

Yield: Serves 4

Ingredients:

4 cups (800 g) plain, low-fat or full-fat Greek yogurt

1 teaspoon chia seeds

Optional Mix-Ins:

Hemp hearts

Cashew butter or nut butter of choice

Coconut shreds

Frozen raspberries

Fresh kiwi (or any fresh fruit you choose)

Granola

Cacao nibs

Chia jam

Bee pollen

1. In a medium bowl, combine the yogurt with the chia seeds.

2. In a drinking glass or parfait cup, layer the yogurt with any mix-ins you choose. Or you can spoon the yogurt mixture into a bowl and top with the mix-ins.

Note: *I also like to serve this on a board, family style, with the different components in different bowls. Then people can serve and top a bowl for themselves.*

Chapter 3

Substantial Salads and Bowls

Rainbow Salad

Yes, this is a salad "recipe," but I encourage you to be flexible on everything but the dressing! This, in other words, is a shop-your-fridge kind of situation. I typically include ingredients such as tomato, radish, carrot, yellow bell pepper, arugula, cucumber, and avocado. Then I boost the flavor with ingredients such as kalamata olives, fresh herbs (especially cilantro and flat-leaf parsley), dried or fresh blueberries, and chopped shallots. Sprouted seeds, such as pumpkin seeds, are thrown in for a delicious crunch. Anchored by the warm grains and topped with a tart fermented kraut (or similar), you can really taste the rainbow.

About that dressing: At the core it's a honey mustard vinaigrette. But over the years I've dialed it in with the exact ingredients and herbs I like.

Yield: Serves 4

Ingredients for the Dressing:

¼ cup (59 ml) extra-virgin olive oil

Juice of ½ lemon

1 tablespoon (15 ml) apple cider vinegar

½ teaspoon raw honey

1 teaspoon spicy brown mustard

¼ teaspoon dried oregano

2 cloves garlic, pressed

Sea salt and black pepper, to taste

Ingredients for the Chopped Salad:

2 cups (360 g) uncooked quinoa

2 big handfuls of arugula, chopped

1 medium shallot, minced

1 cup (200 g) diced cherry tomatoes

1 cup (90 g) shredded carrots

1 large yellow bell pepper, diced

2 small or 1 medium cucumber, diced

¼ cup (180 g) sliced kalamata olives, or to taste

Handful of fresh cilantro leaves, chopped

1–2 tablespoons (4–8 g) chopped fresh flat-leaf parsley

Optional Toppings:

Sliced avocado, sauerkraut, crumbled goat cheese

Make the Dressing:

1. In a large mixing or serving bowl, whisk together all the dressing ingredients.

Note: *I like to make the dressing in a large bowl, then add everything in stages, tossing to combine. If you have trouble whisking the dressing in a large bowl, you can certainly make it in something smaller, add the salad ingredients to a large bowl, then toss with the dressing.*

Make the Chopped Salad:

1. In a small saucepan with a lid, add the quinoa and a scant 2 cups (480 ml) of water. Bring to a boil, reduce the heat to simmer, cover, and cook for 12 minutes.

2. While the quinoa is cooking, to the bowl with the dressing, add the arugula, shallots, cherry tomatoes, carrots, bell peppers, cucumbers, olives, and cilantro. Toss gently to coat evenly.

3. Add the hot quinoa, and toss gently to mix.

4. If you like, top the salad with avocado, sauerkraut, or crumbled goat cheese.

Hearty Sprouted Grains Bowl

I think we all have those Tuesdays or Wednesdays where we look ahead to the next day and, heck, there's just no plan! This dish is great for those days. You can make it truly last minute, but if you do realize your predicament the night before, take advantage and soak those lentils. From there, it's super easy. The next day, you cook the lentils, make a super-simple sauce, and pick your mix-ins based on the season or what's in your fridge. It's a high-fiber dish, and along with Toasty Rice (see 66), it's a full-on meal.

Yield: Serves 4

Ingredients for the Lentils:
2–3 cups (420–630 g) lentils, soaked overnight (page 153) or sprouted (page 20)
1 teaspoon sea salt

Ingredients for the Dressing:
2 tablespoons (30 ml) extra-virgin olive oil
1 teaspoon apple cider vinegar
Zest and juice of 1 lemon
1 teaspoon raw honey
1 clove garlic, pressed
¼ teaspoon dried oregano
⅛ teaspoon ground mustard

Ingredients for the Bowl:
1 large or 2 medium apples, diced small
1 medium red bell pepper, diced
1 stalk celery, minced
1 medium shallot, minced
¼–½ cup (30–60 g) sprouted pumpkin or sunflower seeds
Toasty Rice (recipe follows)

Make the Lentils:

1. In a medium saucepan, add the lentils and salt. Pour in enough water to just cover the lentils.

2. Cook over medium heat for around 20 minutes until the lentils are tender and most of the liquid is absorbed.

Make the Dressing:

1. In a large bowl, whisk together all the ingredients.

Assemble the Bowl:

1. In a bowl, combine the apples, bell peppers, celery, and shallots (or whatever mix-ins you choose). Toss with the sprouted seeds.

2. In a large serving bowl, or individual bowls, assemble the lentils, Toasty Rice, and mix-ins. Drizzle over the dressing.

continued on following page

substantial salads and bowls

For Serving:

Sliced avocado

Pickled Red Onions (page 144)

Fermented pickle slices

Raw sauerkraut

Crumbled feta or goat cheese,
   or your favorite cheese

3. Top with avocado and pickled red onions. And add some fermented pickles or raw sauerkraut for extra tang and crunch, and a good helping of beneficial probiotics. Sprinkle over crumbled feta, goat cheese, or your favorite cheese.

Toasty Rice

Yield: Makes 3 cups cooked

Ingredients:

1 tablespoon (15 ml) olive oil

1 cup (180 g) white rice, soaked,
   rinsed, and drained (see page 20)

2 cups (473 ml) water

Pinch of sea salt

1–2 tablespoons (14–28 g) salted
   butter

1. In a 10-inch (25-cm) sauté pan with a lid, heat the oil over medium-low heat.

2. Add the soaked, rinsed, and drained white rice. Stir occasionally, toasting the rice for several minutes until the liquid is evaporated and the grains have a light, golden color and a slightly nutty smell.

3. Add the water and a generous pinch of salt. Bring to a boil.

4. Add the butter, lower to a simmer, and cover with the lid. Continue to cook over low heat, covered, for 12 minutes.

5. Fluff with a fork and serve.

Note: *Instead of making Toasty Rice, you can cook your favorite rice (preferably sprouted rice or rice you've soaked overnight and rinsed and drained) in the pressure cooker with an equal amount of liquid like Bone Broth (page 149) or water, or a combination of the two. Cook on high pressure for 11 minutes. Feel free to double this recipe, if desired, as one would likely only serve four people.*

Deli-Style Macaroni Salad

Like the White Bean and Bacon Salad (page 70), this is a recipe I make a lot when hosting or bringing something to a gathering table. What's wonderful about this salad is how unique it is for a gluten-free dish. Even in a world that is much more gluten-free friendly, I usually can't find gluten-free premade macaroni salad at the store—and even if you do, so many have excess and oftentimes unhealthy ingredients for a salad that should be so simple.

Trust me when I say this is better than store-bought and worth the work. Also, if you are able to do it, go for the real fermented pickle juice for additional complexity—the salad won't taste like pickles! If you love it, you can make this more of a centerpiece of a meal by adding grilled chicken, or you can customize with more veggies or toppings (see the optional toppings below for my family's go-tos).

Yield: Serves 4

Ingredients for the Sauce:

1 cup (237 ml) mayonnaise (store-bought or homemade, page 69)

1 cup (237 ml) sour cream or plain coconut yogurt (for dairy-free)

¼ cup (59 ml) apple cider vinegar or pickle juice (I prefer real fermented pickles, such as Bubbies.)

2 tablespoons (30 ml) coconut sugar or raw honey

1 tablespoon (15 ml) celery seed

½ teaspoon sea salt

¼ teaspoon black pepper

Ingredients for the Pasta Salad:

1 box (12 ounces, or 340 g) gluten-free elbow macaroni or similar shaped pasta

1 medium red bell pepper, finely diced

2–3 stalks celery, leaves and all, finely diced

Additional, Optional Toppings:

Sliced black olives

Shredded carrot

Chopped tomatoes

Shredded or cubed cooked chicken

Make the Sauce:

1. In a medium bowl, whisk together all the sauce ingredients.

Make the Pasta Salad:

1. In a large pot of boiling salted water, cook the pasta according to the package directions. Place in a colander, rinse under cold water, and drain well. Transfer to a large bowl.

2. Add the bell peppers and celery, and toss well to combine. Pour over the sauce, and gently mix until everything is nicely coated.

3. Place the pasta salad in the refrigerator to chill before serving.

One-Minute Mayo

Yield: Makes about 1 cup

Ingredients:

1 large egg

1 tablespoon (15 ml) fresh lemon
juice (from ½ a small lemon)

1 teaspoon apple cider vinegar or
white vinegar

1 teaspoon yellow or Dijon mustard

¼ teaspoon sea salt

¼ teaspoon coconut sugar or honey

1 cup (237 ml) avocado oil

1. In a jar slightly wider than the head of an immersion blender, add everything—be sure to add the oil last and add it slowly.

2. Insert the immersion blender and have it cover the egg and touch the bottom of the jar.

3. Hold the jar with one hand and turn on the immersion blender. Blend at the bottom of the jar for 20 to 30 seconds until the mixture begins to emulsify—do not move up and down!

4. Once it's turning thick and white, begin to move slowly up the mixture with the blender. Keep moving slowly up until fully emulsified. The whole thing takes about 1 minute.

Note: *If you're looking for a healthier store-bought mayo option, my favorite is Chosen Foods brand avocado oil mayo.*

substantial salads and bowls

69

White Bean and Bacon Salad

This is a super good side that, despite humble ingredients, can even stand out at a potluck. I used to make it with pinto beans, but after switching to cannellini beans I've never looked back. They are the only bean that feels both light and rich to me, which is perfect with the bacon and dressing. (Cannellini beans are also packed with fiber and a great source of minerals such as iron and folate.)

Yield: Serves 4

Ingredients for the Dressing:

¼ cup (59 ml) extra-virgin olive oil

Zest and juice of 1 lemon

1 tablespoon (15 ml) apple cider vinegar

1 medium shallot, minced

¼ teaspoon sea salt

¼ teaspoon black pepper

1 clove garlic, pressed

1 teaspoon raw honey

Ingredients for the Salad:

4 cups (510–680 g) cooked cannellini beans, or 2 cans (15 ounces, or 425 g each), drained and rinsed

1 teaspoon sea salt

1 bay leaf

6 slices pastured bacon, sliced

2 cups (160 g) coarsely chopped arugula

2 tablespoons (8 g) finely minced fresh flat-leaf parsley

½ cup (40 g) shaved Parmesan cheese, plus more for serving

Make the Dressing:

1. In a large bowl, whisk together all the dressing ingredients.

Make the Salad:

1. If cooking cannellini beans from scratch, add the soaked beans to an Instant Pot with enough water to cover. Add the salt and bay leaf. If beans are already cooked, just drain and rinse. Do not cook again.

2. Cover and seal. Cook on high pressure for 25 minutes.

3. Meanwhile, line a plate with a paper towel. In a medium skillet, cook the bacon pieces over medium heat. (You can also cook the bacon in a 400°F (200°C) oven for 15 to 20 minutes; see page 53.) Remove the bacon to the lined plate to drain and cool.

4. Rinse and drain the beans, making sure to remove all excess liquid to avoid a mushy salad. Add the beans to the bowl with the dressing. Toss gently.

5. Add the arugula and parsley leaves, and toss again. Add the Parmesan, and toss to combine.

6. Just before serving, add some of the bacon, reserving a little for sprinkling on the top, and toss again.

7. Top the salad with more Parmesan and the remaining bacon.

Sonoma-Style Chicken Salad Bowl

This is based on the classic chicken salad that features grapes and a creamy dressing. Many versions also have nuts or poppy seeds, though I don't put them in mine. My family loves this style of salad so much that I suppose it was only a matter of time until we realized we could make it a full meal by adding pasta. Now we'll pack it in a reusable container and head down to the beach for a picnic. Note: Feel free to make the chicken salad ahead of time, then cook and add the pasta a day or two later. This works especially well if you're traveling. Note that you can omit the noodles, if you want the chicken salad recipe by itself, or if you want to use it other ways, such as with crackers or on a sandwich.

Yield: Serves 4

Ingredients for the Dressing:

¼ cup (52 g) mayonnaise (store-bought or homemade, page 69)

¼ cup (60 g) sour cream

½ teaspoon onion powder

½ teaspoon garlic powder

¼ teaspoon ground coriander

1 teaspoon sea salt

¼ teaspoon black pepper

Juice of 1 small lemon

Ingredients for the Pasta Salad:

1 box (12 ounces, or 340 g) gluten-free fusilli noodles or your favorite noodles

1 pound (454 g) chicken breast, cooked, cubed or shredded

3 stalks celery, finely minced

1 medium shallot, finely minced

2–3 cups (474–711 g) red grapes, halved

Optional:

Handful of fresh flat-leaf parsley, chopped

½ cup (35 g) sliced almonds or sprouted pumpkin seeds

Make the Dressing:

1. In a large bowl, whisk to combine all the dressing ingredients.

Make the Pasta Salad:

1. In a large pot of boiling salted water, cook the pasta according to the package directions. Drain and rinse with cool water.

2. To the bowl with the dressing, add the cooked and drained pasta, cooked chicken, celery, shallots, and grapes. Toss well to combine. If you like, add some parsley along with sliced almonds or sprouted seeds.

3. Serve warm, room temperature, or chilled with a sprinkle of parsley on top, if desired.

Taco Salad with Catalina Dressing

It was years ago when a family friend introduced us to using Catalina on this style of salad. Of course, the store-bought version has its issues with ingredients—sugars, gums, oils I try to avoid, and often food coloring as well. What I love about using it on taco salad is that the sweet and vinegary nature of the dressing reminds me of a tangy taco sauce in a way.

Yield: Serves 4

Ingredients for the Dressing:

1 cup (237 ml) extra-virgin olive oil

½ cup (118 ml) red wine vinegar

½ cup (118 ml) ketchup

1 teaspoon onion powder

1 teaspoon paprika

½ teaspoon Worcestershire sauce

⅓–½ cup (79–118 ml) raw honey

½–1 teaspoon sea salt

Black pepper, to taste

Ingredients for the Salad:

1 pound (454 g) pasture-raised ground beef or ground turkey, or 2 cups (420 g) lentils

1 medium yellow onion, diced

3–5 cloves garlic, pressed

2 tablespoons (30 ml) taco seasoning (store-bought or homemade, page 148)

1 teaspoon tomato paste

¼ cup (59 ml) water or Bone Broth (page 149)

Sea salt and black pepper, to taste

2 cups (342 g) cooked sprouted pinto beans (see page 21) or canned pinto beans, rinsed

4–6 cups (188–282 g) chopped lettuces (I used a combination of chopped Romaine and shredded cabbage.)

2 cups (360 g) halved or quartered grape or cherry tomatoes

Shredded raw Cheddar cheese

Chopped fresh cilantro

Cubed avocado

Crushed corn chips

Make the Dressing:

1. In a blender or food processor, combine all the dressing ingredients and blend until smooth. Taste and adjust seasoning as needed.

Make the Salad:

1. In a 10-inch (25-cm) skillet set over medium heat, cook the ground meat until no longer pink, or cook the lentils until tender.

2. Add the onions, garlic, taco seasoning, tomato paste, water, salt, and pepper. Sauté until the onions are tender and the liquid has been absorbed.

3. In a large bowl, add the lettuces. Top with the taco meat or lentil blend, tomatoes, cheese, cilantro, and avocado and corn chips if you like.

4. Drizzle over some of the homemade Catalina dressing—we drizzle the heck out of it!—and serve.

How to Store: *The dressing keeps in the fridge for a week or so. It makes about 3 cups (720 ml), which is more than enough for the salad.*

Tip: *You can add diced potatoes to your protein to stretch things further, and it's a delicious addition.*

Mediterranean-Style Pasta Salad

I guess deep down I am a pasta salad lover because in addition to the Deli-Style Macaroni Salad (page 67), this is another classic salad that I needed to reverse engineer after going gluten-free (and once I started reading labels seriously). There is a good amount of variation in different recipes, but you know the kind of salad it is if you've had it before: cucumber, cherry tomato, roasted red peppers (or sun-dried tomatoes), kalamata olives, and sometimes artichoke hearts. It's now frequently in the weekend lunch rotation at our house.

Yield: Serves 4

Ingredients for the Dressing:

¼ cup (59 ml) red wine vinegar or apple cider vinegar

⅔ cup (158 ml) extra-virgin olive oil

3 tablespoons (44 ml) mayonnaise (store-bought or homemade, page 69)

1–3 cloves garlic

½ teaspoon dried basil

½ teaspoon dried oregano

1 teaspoon raw honey

Sea salt and black pepper, to taste

Ingredients for the Pasta Salad:

1 box (12 ounces, or 340 g) gluten-free fusilli or your favorite pasta

1 large cucumber, quartered length-wise and thinly sliced

2 cups (360 g) halved or quartered grape or cherry tomatoes

1–2 medium bell peppers, diced

3–4 roasted red peppers, diced

2 shallots or 1 medium red onion, thinly sliced

1 cup (180 g) sliced black olives or kalamata olives

1 cup (180 g) sliced green olives

1 jar or can (8 ounces, or 227 g) quartered artichoke hearts

Make the Dressing:

1. To a blender, add all the dressing ingredients. Blend until smooth.

2. Pour the dressing into the bottom of a large bowl.

Make the Pasta Salad:

1. In a large pot of boiling salted water, cook the pasta according to the package directions. Drain and rinse with cool water.

2. To the bowl with the dressing, add the cooked and drained pasta along with the remaining ingredients. Toss it all together gently.

3. Taste and adjust the seasoning if necessary. Serve warm, room temperature, or chilled.

Tip: *This pasta salad keeps well, so it's fine to make a day ahead and refrigerate.*

Note: *If you want to make it a meal, add diced grilled chicken thighs that have been marinated in a mixture of olive oil, dried basil, dried oregano, crushed red pepper, fresh crushed garlic, and the juice of one lemon. It's best to marinate in the refrigerator at least a couple hours for maximum flavor. Grill the chicken, then let it rest for about 5 minutes. Dice it and add it to your pasta salad.*

substantial salads and bowls

Roasted Asparagus and Pecan Salad

This salad has a wonderful balsamic dressing. Together with the dried cranberries you get a wonderful sweet-tart character that marries well with the savory roasted asparagus. I originally made it on a whim with a bunch of asparagus to use up. When remaking it and retooling it, what eventually took it to the next level was the pecans for crunch and the funky goat cheese (which is a classic with cranberries!). That said, if you have those who don't like goat cheese in your house, feta works well too.

Yield: Serves 4 to 6

Ingredients for the Dressing:

¼ cup (59 ml) extra-virgin olive oil

3 tablespoons (44 ml) balsamic vinegar

2 teaspoons Dijon mustard

1 tablespoon (15 ml) raw honey

1–2 cloves garlic, pressed

¼ teaspoon sea salt

¼ teaspoon black pepper

Ingredients for the Salad:

1 pound (454 g) asparagus, trimmed

1 tablespoon (15 ml) extra-virgin olive oil

Sea salt and black pepper, to taste

⅔ cup (120 g) halved cherry tomatoes

¼ cup (30 g) dried cranberries

⅔ cup (83 g) coarsely chopped pecans, divided

Feta or goat cheese for sprinkling on top

Make the Dressing:

1. In a large bowl, whisk together all the dressing ingredients.

Make the Salad:

1. Preheat the oven to 400°F (200°C). Line a baking sheet with parchment paper.

2. In a large bowl, gently toss the asparagus in the olive oil. Season with salt and pepper to taste. Lay the asparagus on the baking sheet and roast for 12 to 15 minutes until it's tender with a hint of crunch. Set aside until it's cool enough to handle, then cut into bite-size pieces.

3. To the bowl with the dressing, add the asparagus, tomatoes, dried cranberries, and some of the pecans. Toss gently to combine.

4. Sprinkle the salad with cheese and the remaining pecans.

Cranberries by the Handful

Blueberries and other snacking berries tend to get more attention, but cranberries are a powerful food when it comes to antioxidants as well. It's well known that they may help with urinary tract health, but they may also promote skin and heart health. They have antibacterial properties as well. Those are plenty of reasons to snack on a small handful of dried cranberries while you make this recipe!

Fresh Thai-Style Salad

We love Thai lettuce cups. This recipe is basically everything you'd use for that but with noodles mixed in. It is delicious, nourishing, and so nice for a warm summer evening. I most often use cashew butter for the sauce, but peanut butter is of course the classic choice with this dish. If you're nut-free, tahini or sun butter would be delicious too.

Yield: Serves 4

Ingredients for the Sauce:

About 1 cup (237 ml) nut butter

Zest and juice of 2 limes

Optional: 1 teaspoon sriracha

2-inch (5-cm) piece fresh ginger, grated

2 cloves garlic, pressed

2 tablespoons (30 ml) raw honey

2 tablespoons (30 ml) coconut aminos

¼ cup (59 ml) water

1 tablespoon (15 ml) sesame oil

Sea salt, to taste

Ingredients for the Salad:

1 package (8 ounces, or 227 g) pad Thai rice noodles

1 medium carrot

1 medium red bell pepper

½ of a green cabbage

½ of a purple cabbage

1–2 medium radishes

For Serving:

3 scallions, white and green parts, chopped

1 cup (64 g) chopped fresh cilantro

2 cups (104 g) mung bean sprouts

Optional:

Chopped peanuts or cashews

Lime wedges

Sriracha

Make the Sauce:

1. In a blender or food processor, add all the sauce ingredients and process until smooth. Set aside.

Make the Salad:

1. Cook the rice noodles according to the package directions. Drain well.

2. Shred, spiralize, or julienne the vegetables.

Assemble:

1. In a large bowl, combine the cooked and drained noodles with the vegetables. Add the sauce, and toss to coat everything evenly.

2. Top with the scallions, cilantro, and bean sprouts, and a sprinkling of nuts if using. Serve with lime wedges and sriracha on the side.

substantial salads and bowls

Chopped Antipasto with Crispy Prosciutto

This is a pizza place classic with lettuce, deli meat, and onion. I always wanted that but with better-quality ingredients . . . and more good stuff! I'm talking great quality meat, raw flavorful cheeses, and why not add some beans and artichoke hearts for texture and flavor? The dressing is a bracing Italian vinaigrette. Use good-quality oil and vinegar, and you can't go wrong.

Yield: Serves 4

Ingredients for the Dressing:

¼ cup (59 ml) extra-virgin olive oil

2 tablespoons (30 ml) red wine vinegar

2 cloves garlic, pressed

½ teaspoon sea salt

½ teaspoon dried thyme

½ teaspoon dried oregano

¼ teaspoon black pepper

¼ teaspoon onion powder

¼ teaspoon ground mustard

Ingredients for the Salad:

2 big handfuls (2½ ounces, or 71 g) arugula, chopped

2 big handfuls (2½ ounces, or 71 g) Romaine lettuce, chopped

½ cup (8 g) fresh flat-leaf parsley, chopped

1 cup (180 g) diced cherry or grape tomatoes

1–2 medium shallots, quartered and thinly sliced

¾ cup (99 g) cubed raw Cheddar or mozzarella cheese

6 slices (3 ounces, or 85 g) prosciutto, cooked until crispy

2 ounces (57 g) uncured salami

¼ cup (30 g) thinly sliced pepperoncini

½ cup (57 g) kalamata olives

1 cup (164 g) garbanzo beans, drained if canned

½ cup (84 g) artichoke hearts or hearts of palm

Make the Dressing:

1. In the bottom of a big salad bowl, whisk together all the dressing ingredients to emulsify.

Make the Salad:

1. Add all the salad ingredients to the dressing. Toss well to combine.

Tip: *If you prefer a heavily dressed salad—or want to keep extra in the fridge—double or triple the dressing recipe. It will keep for up to 1 week in the refrigerator.*

Tip: *An easy way to cook the prosciutto is in a 350°F (175°C) oven for 12 to 15 minutes. Just keep an eye on them to make sure they don't burn.*

Sushi Roll in a Bowl

Sushi is so expensive. It's easy to spend as much on one person's dinner as you spend on a meal like this to feed a family. And this is a whole-family hit: Kids love this meal because it's got that finger food appeal. Each bite can be different, and you can use the nori to scoop up bites. While it is of course delicious with fresh salmon, don't shy away from canned. In our house we will make this on the fly with canned salmon, and it's still so good.

Yield: Makes 1 bowl

Ingredients:

1 cup (237 ml) water

½ cup (90 g) rice

2 tablespoons (30 ml) toasted sesame oil

2 tablespoons (30 ml) coconut aminos

8 tablespoons (120 ml) rice vinegar, divided

¾ teaspoon sea salt, divided

1 cup (133 g) diced English or Persian cucumber

Sesame seeds, to taste

½ teaspoon raw honey

1 can (5 ounces, or 142 g) salmon or any fresh/canned fish of choice, drained

½ avocado, sliced

1 tablespoon (7 g) or more furikake (I like Muso from Japan brand.)

1–2 packages nori or dried seaweed (5 g each)

Optional Toppings:

Micro cilantro

Pickled red onion

Pickled ginger

Yellowbird jalapeño hot sauce

1. Cook the rice: In a medium pot, bring the water to a boil. Add the rice, and lower the heat to a simmer. Cover and cook for 12 minutes.

2. Meanwhile, in a small saucepan, heat up the sesame oil, coconut aminos, 1 tablespoon (15 ml) of rice vinegar, and ⅛ teaspoon of salt. Simmer until thick, 4 to 7 minutes.

3. Place the cucumber in a small mixing bowl and drizzle 3 tablespoons (44 ml) of rice vinegar over it to coat. Add ⅛ teaspoon of salt and as much sesame seed as you like. Mix to combine.

4. To turn your rice into more of a sushi rice, in a measuring cup, whisk together 4 tablespoons (59 ml) of rice vinegar, the honey, and ¼ teaspoon salt. Pour that over your cooked rice, and stir to combine.

5. Build your bowl! Place the salmon in the bowl and drizzle over the thickened sauce. Add the cucumbers and rice, and top it with avocado and PLENTY of furikake, if you're obsessed like I am. (Plus it's beautiful.) Add other toppings if you like.

6. Serve with nori to build your sushi bites as you go.

Note: *This recipe yield is what I make for myself, which results in one giant bowl. Feel free to scale as needed.*

Kid-Friendly Taco Boats

This is one of my son, Ezekiel's favorites to the point where we have had it every year at his birthday party. Taco bowls, fruit, lemonade, and cupcakes . . . okay, even I agree it doesn't get much better than that! Now, there was quite the controversy on social media when I first posted about this recipe because depending on where you live in the country, it can be called by other names (Walking Tacos, Taco in a Bag), and it fired people up! But eventually everyone agreed that no matter the name, this is a crowd-pleaser for just about anyone and nearly any age.

Yield: Serves 4+

Ingredients:

1 bag (10 ounces, or 283 g) corn chips or tortilla chips

4–6 cups Gigi's Blue Ribbon Chili (page 102) or similar, hot

½ head iceberg or other crisp lettuce, shredded

1 cup (115 g) shredded raw Cheddar cheese

1 cup (180 g) diced tomatoes

¾–1 cup (177–237 ml) Buttermilk Ranch (recipe follows)

1. Line the bottom of 4–6 kraft paper bowls with the chips. (Okay, sure you can use regular bowls but it's not the same!)

2. Top each bowl with a portion of the chili.

3. Divide up and sprinkle over the lettuce, cheese, and tomatoes.

4. Drizzle ranch over the top of each bowl.

Buttermilk Ranch

Make sure to blend the herbs first or you will end up with green ranch. Trust me.

Yield: Makes about 1+ cups; Serves 6+

Ingredients:

Handful of fresh flat-leaf parsley leaves

About ¼ cup (2 g) fresh dill

½ cup (120 g) sour cream

½ cup (104 g) mayonnaise (store-bought or homemade, page 69)

½ cup (118 ml) buttermilk

1 teaspoon apple cider vinegar

1 teaspoon Worcestershire sauce

½ teaspoon garlic powder

¼ teaspoon onion powder

¼ teaspoon sea salt

¼ teaspoon black pepper

1. In a food processor, blender, or by hand, finely chop the parsley and dill.

2. To the herbs, fold in the sour cream. Add the remaining ingredients, and mix gently to combine.

Chapter 4

Warming Soups and Stews

Hearty, Creamy Tomato Soup

If you're of a certain age, then you no doubt remember the classic canned, sometimes even condensed, tomato soup. As I started eating A Little Less Toxic, I switched, of course, to a "healthier" organic version in a box. But in addition to being spendy, it still had manufactured flavor, sodium citrate, and a lot of sugar. This recipe is my answer. Instead of being full of fillers, it is full of tomatoes, spices, and just the right amount of cream (which you can omit for a dairy-free version). About that: My family likes that you can customize the amount of cream even at the last minute. Yes, you can even place a creamer on the table to let each person adjust their own. Pair it with a grilled cheese or make it the center-piece of a dinner with some good crusty bread.

Yield: Serves 4

Ingredients:

1–2 tablespoons (14–28 g) salted butter or extra-virgin olive oil

1 medium yellow onion, diced

1 medium carrot, diced

3–5 cloves garlic, pressed

¼ teaspoon ground turmeric

2 tablespoons (30 ml) tomato paste

2 jars (18 ounces, or 28 g) whole, diced, or crushed tomatoes

3 cups (720 ml) vegetable or chicken broth or Bone Broth (page 149)

⅛ teaspoon ground mustard

⅛ teaspoon ground coriander

Pinch of cayenne pepper

½ teaspoon dried thyme

¼ teaspoon paprika

¼ teaspoon garlic powder

¼ teaspoon onion powder

3–4 bay leaves

1¼ teaspoons sea salt, or to taste

¼ teaspoon black pepper, or to taste

1¼ cups (296 ml) raw cream or heavy cream

For Serving:

¼ cup (59 ml) raw cream or heavy cream

Optional:

Fresh basil cut into ribbons or chopped fresh flat-leaf parsley

Freshly grated Parmesan cheese

1. In a heavy bottom 6- to 8-quart (5.7- to 7.6-L) stockpot, heat the butter over medium heat. Add the onions and carrots, and sauté until tender.

2. Add the garlic, and sauté for 1 to 2 minutes.

3. Make a well in the center of the pan, and add the turmeric and toast for 1 to 2 minutes. Stir to combine.

4. Make a well in the center again, and add the tomato paste. Toast for 2 minutes in the fat, then stir to combine.

5. Add the remaining ingredients except the cream. Bring to a boil, then lower to a simmer. Simmer for at least 20 minutes.

6. Remove the bay leaves, and blend the soup until smooth with immersion blender. Alternatively, you can transfer to a blender.

7. Add the bay leaves back in, and add 1 cup (59 ml) of the heavy cream. Simmer for 10 minutes, stirring occasionally. Remove the bay leaves before serving (or let the "lucky" eaters discover them).

8. Ladle into individual bowls, and serve with a drizzle of the remaining cream on top. Add a sprinkle of basil or parsley, if using, and Parmesan.

Sprouted Lentil Soup with Spinach

My grandma always made a lentil soup in her small apartment kitchen. She was such a good cook, and I'm nostalgic for that soup even though I admit I can't remember many details. These days, we're a soup-loving family. But one thing's for sure: Lentil soup is one food I will absolutely not buy premade. It's less to do with the ingredients, as you can find organic versions without the worst offenders, but the sodium in even the best store-bought soups is high, and the texture is just never perfect on the lentils!

Thanks to the cumin, my soup is almost a little smoky, but not overpowering. It comes across to most people as earthy, warm, and hearty. Now, back to the texture: The lentils are quite soft, but they still have a little bite to them. It's not exactly a crunch, but they hold their shape until you bite them, then they break down easily as soon as you start chewing. Enjoy it with your family, or pack it in quart-size mason jars to drop it off to someone who needs a restorative meal!

Yield: Serves 4

Ingredients:

2 tablespoons (30 ml) extra-virgin olive oil

1 medium yellow onion, diced

3–4 stalks celery, diced

3 medium carrots, diced

3–4 cloves garlic, pressed

¼ teaspoon ground turmeric

1 jar (18 ounces, or 510 g) diced tomatoes

1 tablespoon (15 ml) apple cider vinegar

4 cups (840 g) dried lentils, soaked overnight and drained (even better if sprouted)

1 quart (1 L) vegetable broth or Bone Broth (page 149)

3–4 cups (468–624 g) frozen spinach

¼ teaspoon paprika

1 tablespoon (15 ml) ground cumin

1 tablespoon (15 ml) dried oregano

1 tablespoon (15 ml) dried basil

Pinch of crushed red pepper

3–4 bay leaves

2 quarts (2 L) water

1. In a heavy bottom 8-quart (7.6-L) stockpot, heat the olive oil over medium-low heat. Add the onions, celery, and carrots, and sauté for about 5 minutes until tender.

2. Add the garlic, and sauté for 1 to 2 minutes.

3. Make a well in the center of the pan, add the turmeric, and toast for 1 to 2 minutes, then stir to combine.

4. Add the remaining ingredients. Bring to a boil, then lower the heat to a simmer. Simmer uncovered for about 30 minutes until the lentils are cooked.

5. Remove the bay leaves before serving.

Note: *This is also a great one to make in a slow cooker (see page 94).*

continued on following page

Slow Cooker Instructions: *Toss every-thing in the slow cooker. Cook on low for 6 to 8 hours or high for 4 to 5 hours. You can also add all these ingredients to a freezer-safe airtight storage container and freeze for up to 4 months. When ready to use, move the frozen container to the refrigerator overnight, dump the contents into the slow cooker in the morning, turn the slow cooker on low, and dinner is ready later!*

Tip: *I love to make this with small meatballs sometimes, too. Use my Grain-Free Meatball recipe (page 170) with whatever ground meat you like—we like beef best in this—and form into marble-size meatballs. Add them to the pot while the soup is on a low boil. (I like to add them in a clockwise rotation at the hour intervals of a clock, so I remember where I added my previous meatball, preventing them from sticking together.) Simmer for 7 to 10 minutes once all the meatballs are in the pot to finish cooking them.*

Damien's Mineral-Rich Chicken Noodle Soup

Damien grew up eating all sorts of things that I didn't. So maybe it's no surprise that his version of a "classic" chicken noodle has rutabaga and a whole cabbage in it. He grew up watching his mom and grandma cook (and his grandma was an old-school Slovakian-style cook at that).

Anyways, at some point in our joint cooking journey we realized we didn't have a go-to chicken noodle soup, and we desperately needed it. It's a comfort food, rainy-day food, a not-feeling-well food. Thanks to Damien, we now have just the soup, full of complete healing goodness.

For the noodles I use Jovial gluten-free noodles, but I don't add the noodles to the soup pot as they can become mushy over time, and we eat this for multiple days or freeze extra to have another day. So, I make the noodles separately and serve the hot soup over the cooked and strained noodles.

Yield: Serves 4

Ingredients:

1 teaspoon avocado oil or fat of choice

4–5 medium carrots, diced

4–5 stalks celery, sliced

1 medium yellow onion, diced

⅛–¼ teaspoon ground turmeric

4–5 cloves garlic, pressed

1 quart (1 L) chicken broth or Bone Broth (page 149)

1 (4–5 pound [1.8–2.3 kg]) whole chicken

1 cup (140 g) peeled and diced rutabaga

1 whole small- to medium-size green cabbage, cored and chopped

2–3 leeks, washed and chopped

2 bay leaves

Sea salt and black pepper, to taste

¼ teaspoon ground mustard

⅛ teaspoon ground coriander

½ teaspoon paprika

½ teaspoon lemon pepper seasoning

½ teaspoon garlic powder

½ teaspoon onion powder

Optional:
Cooked noodles (My favorite is fusilli.)

continued on following page

1. In a giant stockpot large enough to fit your whole bird plus other ingredients (I use a 16 quart [15 L]), heat the oil over medium heat. Add the carrots, celery, and onions. Sauté for about 5 minutes until tender.

2. Make a well in the middle of the pan, add a little more oil, then add the turmeric, and toast for a minute or two.

3. Add the garlic, and sauté for a minute. Add the broth along with the whole bird.

4. Add the remaining veggies, and season with all the spices. Cover with water, and bring to a boil. Lower to a simmer and cook for 1 to 3 or more hours. (A longer simmer makes a richer broth.)

5. Remove the chicken, making sure you get all the bones out. Place it on a cutting board; when cool enough to handle, carefully remove the meat and roughly chop. The bones and skin can be saved and used to make more bone broth later. Return the chicken to the soup.

6. Taste the soup and adjust the seasonings, if needed. Serve over freshly made noodles, if desired.

One-Pot Beef Stew with Chiles and Carrots

This is a beef stew that's hard to describe as it was inspired by various versions I've had over the years. It's hearty and so rich it's almost creamy. It's warming thanks to all the spices and green chiles. I love serving it in a wide, shallow bowl, with a big scoop of Toasty Rice (page 66) in the center. Sprinkle with a bit of fresh cilantro and enjoy.

Yield: Serves 4

Ingredients:

1 tablespoon (15 ml) olive oil, if searing meat

3 pounds (1.4 kg) beef stew meat, like chuck

1 cup (59 ml) water

2 jars (18 ounces, or 510 g) diced tomatoes

1 medium yellow onion, diced

3 cloves garlic, pressed

2 cans (4 ounces, or 113 g) or 1 can (7 ounces, or 198 g) green chiles (Or use a fresh roasted and seeded poblano.)

1 teaspoon ground cumin

½ teaspoon smoked paprika

⅛ teaspoon ground mustard

⅛ teaspoon ground coriander

1 teaspoon dried oregano

½ teaspoon garlic powder

½ teaspoon onion powder

½ teaspoon chili powder

Sea salt and black pepper, to taste

1 tablespoon (15 ml) tapioca flour

5–10 carrots (depending on size and preference), sliced on the bias, about ½-inch (1.3-cm) thick

Pressure Cooker Method:

1. If you're not pressed for time or feeling fancy, turn the pot to sauté mode (if that option is available), add the olive oil, and let that warm for a minute. Add the meat, and sauté until brown, just a minute or so on each side.

2. Turn off sauté. Add the rest of your ingredients except the tapioca flour and carrots, starting with the water.

3. Close, seal, and pressure-cook on high pressure for 1 hour. Release the pressure at least 20 minutes before the meal needs to be ready.

4. Open the lid and remove about 1 cup (59 ml) of liquid to a oven-safe dish. Whisk in the tapioca flour and return this thickened liquid to the pot. Add the carrots.

5. Close, seal, and pressure-cook on high for 3 minutes. Release the pressure, stir, and serve.

continued on following page

warming soups and stews

Stovetop Method:

1. Heat a heavy-bottomed pot or an enameled cast-iron Dutch oven over medium heat for several minutes until evenly heated.

2. Add the olive oil, and let warm a minute. Add the meat, and brown on each side for just a minute or so. Remove the meat to a separate dish.

3. Add the onions to the hot pot. Sauté for about 5 minutes until tender, scraping up those browned meat bits. Add the garlic during the last minute or 2 of cooking.

4. Return the meat to the pot. Add all the seasonings, and the tomatoes and green chiles.

5. Bring to boil, then lower the heat to a simmer. Cover and simmer for 1 hour.

6. Add the carrots, return the lid, and continue cooking for 15 minutes or so until the carrots are tender.

7. Remove the lid and transfer 1 cup (59 ml) of the liquid to a oven-safe dish. Whisk the tapioca flour into this liquid. Return this thickened liquid to the pot. Continue to simmer for 3 minutes or so until all the sauce has thickened some, stirring occasionally.

Gigi's Blue Ribbon Chili

When I was growing up, my mom's chili was the best. And it wasn't just me that thought so! While it wasn't the county fair, at some point she was definitely the winner of a soup cook-off with her recipe. I wrote it down, of course, though over the years I have made a few adaptations, sprouting the beans, adding toasted turmeric, and using coconut sugar.

This can be served in a variety of ways over several days, or double the recipe to freeze extra for a rainy day. (Doesn't chili always taste better left over?) Use it up on chili fries, chili-loaded baked sweet potatoes, chili Cincinnati, chili with rice—you name it. Or make a big bowl, and top it with diced shallots, scallions, raw Cheddar cheese, and sour cream.

Yield: Makes 10 bowls

Ingredients:

1 tablespoon (15 ml) extra-virgin olive oil, plus more if needed

1 large yellow onion, diced

4–5 cloves garlic, pressed

1 pound (454 g) pasture-raised ground beef or turkey

Sea salt and black pepper, to taste

¼ teaspoon ground turmeric

3 jars (18 ounces, or 510 g) diced tomatoes

4 cups (878 g) cooked kidney, pinto, or black beans or 2 cans (15.5 ounces, or 439 g each) with liquid (You can use a combination.)

3–4 bay leaves

1 tablespoon (15 ml) chili powder

2 teaspoons (5 g) ground cumin

½ teaspoon dried oregano

⅛ teaspoon crushed red pepper

¼ teaspoon ground mustard

1 tablespoon (15 ml) coconut sugar

1. In a large pot, heat the olive oil over medium heat. Add the onions, and sauté for 3 to 5 minutes until translucent, adding the garlic during the last minute of cooking.

2. Add the meat, and cook until browned. Add the salt and pepper, and stir to combine thoroughly.

3. Make a well in the middle of your pot, add a little more oil if needed, sprinkle in the turmeric, and toast for a minute or two. Mix to combine into the meat.

4. Add the tomatoes, beans with the liquid, and all the seasonings. Stir to combine everything well.

5. Heat to a boil, then reduce to a simmer. Cook for 1 hour, stirring occasionally. Don't forget to taste, and add more seasonings if needed.

White Bean Chicken Chili

When my family goes camping, I like to pack something from home for the first night. By the time we drive eight or nine hours it's almost dark. So, I made this at home and freestyled it with the recipe the first time. I packed it in half-gallon mason jars, and we had it with toppings like fresh cilantro and shredded cheese. We were blown away, but didn't know if it was just the reward at the end of a long day. When I made it again at home, I wasn't sure if it would hold up . . . but it did! To this day, it remains a "must pack" recipe for camping trips.

Yield: Serves 4

Ingredients:

6 cups (1.3 kg) cooked cannellini beans or 3 cans (15½ ounces, or 439 g each) with liquid and divided

1 cup (237 ml) water

1–2 tablespoons (15–30 ml) extra-virgin olive oil

1 medium yellow onion, diced

¼ teaspoon ground turmeric

3–4 cloves garlic, pressed

1½–2 pounds (680–908 g) boneless, skinless chicken thighs

1 bunch fresh cilantro, leaves only, chopped (Reserve a handful for serving.)

1 can (7–8 ounces, or 198–227 g) green chilies, diced

3 cups (720 ml) Bone Broth (page 149)

½ teaspoon dried oregano

1 teaspoon chili powder

½ teaspoon ground cumin

¼ teaspoon onion powder

¼ teaspoon garlic powder

3–4 bay leaves

½ teaspoon sea salt

⅛ teaspoon black pepper

For Serving: 1 lime

1. In a blender or food processor, add 1 cup (220 g) of beans with some liquid and the 1 cup (237 ml) of water, and blend until completely combined. Set it aside.

2. In a 6- to 8-quart (5.7- to 7.6-L) pot, heat the oil over medium heat. Add the onions, and sauté until translucent, about 5 minutes.

3. Make a well in the center, add a little more oil if needed, and toast the turmeric for 2 to 3 minutes. Add the garlic, and sauté for 1 to 2 minutes.

4. Add the remaining ingredients, including the beans and their liquid plus the blended beans. Bring to a boil.

5. Cook for 20 to 30 minutes. When the chicken is cooked through, it should reach 165°F [74°C] on a meat thermometer. Remove it and place it on a cutting board. Shred the chicken thighs thoroughly, and add it all back to the pot. Lower the heat to a simmer, and let the chili cook for 30 minutes to 1 hour.

6. Squeeze in the lime juice before serving. Top with fresh cilantro.

Tip: *You can serve the chili with more lime wedges, Cheddar cheese, avocado slices, and hot sauce of your choice. It is also delicious served with corn bread or crispy baked tortilla strips.*

Good to Go

The White Bean Chicken Chili recipe isn't the only one I've experimented with bringing on trips. There's just nothing better than starting a vacation off with a home-cooked meal—especially one that just needs reheating or fresh toppings to serve. Here are a few other hits from over the years.

Meals to Pack for Camping (grill or campfire friendly reheat)

When all you have is a real fire or grill to cook, night one goes best if you don't even have to do much more than light the fire. That means Mason jar meals like Sprouted Lentil Soup with Spinach (page 93), Gigi's Blue Ribbon Chili (page 102), and Aguadito de Pollo with Aji Verde Sauce (page 113) are easy to bring along. Or, for the White Bean and Bacon Salad (page 70), set the bacon aside and combine just before serving. The House Bolognese (page 164) can be packed and poured over fresh noodles made at camp. For breakfast the next day, you can make something at home to pack like the Grain-Free Chocolate Chip Banana Bread (page 49), Next Day Oatmeal Muffins (page 50), or Pressure-Cooked Eggs (page 51). (And don't forget the cold brew, if you partake!) That way day 1 at camp doesn't have to start with more cooking.

Meals to Pack for Hotels (no full kitchen)

This is a tricky one as many rooms will just have a kettle and microwave (which I try to avoid using). Breakfasts to bring would be same as the camp. For cold meals, most of the salads in this book can travel well if you have a quality cooler and hold the dressing until arrival. The Sonoma-Style Chicken Salad Bowl (page 73) with some bread or crackers is a nice arrival snack as well. Or if you are a cold pasta loving person like me, try something like the Pasta Pot (page 163).

Meals to Pack for Rental Homes (full kitchen)

You might be thinking: "If I have a full kitchen, can't I just cook anything in the book?" Well, sure. But still, these are some favorites to make ahead and pack to make the beginning of a trip—before you have all the groceries and the kitchen figured out—more delicious: White Bean and Bacon Salad (page 70), Taco Salad with Catalina Dressing (page 74), Mediterranean-Style Pasta Salad (page 77), One-Pot Beef Stew with Chiles and Carrots (page 99), Sprouted Lentil Soup with Spinach (page 93), White Bean Chicken Chili (page 105), Albóndigas Soup (page 107), and Aguadito de Pollo with Aji Verde Sauce (page 113).

Albóndigas Soup

Many of our local Mexican restaurants serve a small bowl of albóndigas soup before a meal. I realize this is not a widespread thing, but it's similar to getting miso soup at a sushi restaurant. If you've never had the pleasure of albóndigas soup, it has a little smokiness and it's hearty. I've found it's a great soup to serve people who think they aren't soup people! At our house we eat it as a main, rather than an appetizer, and it stands on its own—no sides needed. If you want to level it up, pile on the toppings.

Yield: Serves 4

Ingredients for the Meatballs:

1 pound (454 g) pasture-raised ground beef or meat of choice

1 large egg

½ cup (90 g) white rice (soaked overnight and rinsed well; see page 20)

¼ teaspoon chili powder

¼ teaspoon chipotle powder

½ teaspoon ground cumin

½ teaspoon sea salt

Ingredients for the Soup:

1 tablespoon (15 ml) avocado oil

1 medium yellow onion, diced

4–5 medium carrots, diced

4–5 stalks celery, sliced

¼–½ teaspoon ground turmeric

5 cloves garlic, minced

1 quart (1 L) Bone Broth (homemade, page 149, or store-bought)

1 cup (16 g) fresh cilantro leaves, plus more for garnish

1 jar (18½ ounces, or 524 g) diced tomatoes

1 tablespoon (15 ml) tomato paste

About 1 quart (1 L) water

¼–½ teaspoon garlic powder

¼ teaspoon onion powder

1 teaspoon ground cumin

¼ teaspoon ground coriander

1 teaspoon dried oregano

½ teaspoon paprika

3–4 bay leaves

Optional, for Serving:

Fresh cilantro leaves

Lime wedges

Sliced radish

Sliced avocado

Sliced jalapeño

continued on following page

Make the Meatballs:

In a large bowl, combine all the ingredients. Form into 1-inch (2.5-cm) balls and place them on a plate. I always form the meatballs one at a time and add to the boiling soup as I go. Less dishes and saves time.

Note: *You can do this while the soup is coming to a boil, between steps 2 and 3.*

Make the Soup:

1. In a 6- to 8-quart (5.7- to 7.6-L) pot, heat the oil over medium heat. Add the onions, carrots, and celery, and sauté until tender. Make a well in the middle, add the turmeric, and toast for about 1 to 2 minutes.

2. Add the garlic, and cook for about 1 minute. Add the rest of the soup ingredients and stir gently. Raise the heat to bring the soup to a boil.

3. Once the soup is boiling, add the meatballs, one at a time, making sure not to add a meatball where one was recently added to prevent them from sticking together or breaking apart. Lower to a simmer and partly cover the pot. Cook for 15 minutes.

4. Serve the meatball soup with cilantro, lime wedges, radish, avocado, and jalapeños, if you like.

Optional Add-Ins: *This soup is great as-is, and it is delicious with all kinds of add-ins. Try it with some diced potato, corn, diced zucchini, or fresh spinach—or mix it up with a combination of veggies.*

Red Lentil Dal with Warming Spices

Rice and beans are a classic, low-cost meal. But if you want a recipe that, with some time, heat, and yes, plenty of spices, shows all it can be, this is it. It's rich and flavorful, and honestly it's not like much else in this book when it comes to the flavor profile. It's a stew, but the lentils really cook down to almost a loose, refried-bean texture. Oh, and I do believe beyond being warming, spices are anti-inflammatory and aid in digestion, so those are all good reasons to turn to this meal even when it's warm out.

I usually double this recipe and am able to freeze enough for another meal or two. It's also great served with lamb meatballs using my Grain-Free Meatballs (page 170).

Yield: Serves 4

Ingredients:

2 cups (420 g) red lentils, soaked overnight in water and a splash of apple cider vinegar, drained, and rinsed (Sprouted a day or two is even better.)

2 tablespoons (30 ml) avocado oil, divided

1 medium yellow onion, diced

3–5 cloves garlic, pressed

¾ teaspoon ground cumin

¾ teaspoon chili powder

½ teaspoon paprika

2 bay leaves

A few bruised cardamom pods

1 teaspoon fennel seed

1 teaspoon cumin seed

1 teaspoon fenugreek

1 teaspoon ground turmeric

2 tablespoons (30 ml) freshly grated ginger

2 jars (18 ounces, or 510 g each) diced tomatoes

For Serving:

Toasty Rice (page 66), mixed with 3 to 4 gently pressed cardamom pods

Vegetables of choice (see note)

Fresh cilantro leaves or microgreens

Hot sauce

Optional, for Serving:

Za'atar mixed with a little coarse salt and olive oil for drizzling over

continued on following page

1. In the pressure cooker on sauté mode, heat 1 tablespoon (15 ml) of the avocado oil. Add the onions, and sauté for 3 to 5 minutes until translucent. Turn off the sauté function and immediately add the garlic. Sauté briefly, making sure not to let it burn.

2. Heat a small pan over medium-low heat until very hot. Add the remaining tablespoon (15 ml) of avocado oil, and heat until nice and hot. Add all the spices (cumin through turmeric) and stir, watching closely. When the spices are toasted a bit and fragrant (this takes just a minute or so), add them to the Instant Pot.

3. Add the fresh ginger, soaked lentils, and tomatoes, along with enough water to cover the lentils by about ½ inch (1.3 cm). Put on the lid and set the vent to sealed. Set to high pressure for 25 minutes.

4. Serve the dal with Toasty Rice and whatever vegetable you like. Top with fresh cilantro or microgreens. Serve with hot sauce, za'atar, and olive oil for drizzling over.

Note: *For the veggies, try cooking some chopped zucchini with some thinly sliced shallot in some toasted curry powder in hot avocado oil. Added sumac, salt, and a bit of coconut sugar to balance it out.*

If you want to cook this on the stovetop, follow the same steps to get everything in the pot. Then bring to a boil, stirring frequently, reduce to a simmer, cover, and cook for 20 minutes (no need to stir).

Aguadito de Pollo with Aji Verde Sauce

I remember the night at a local Peruvian restaurant when I fell in love with this soup. Eventually I had to make it at home. And once I figured out a solid recipe, I decided to swap in another Peruvian ingredient, using quinoa instead of rice. It adds protein, so it keeps you full even longer—and I think the texture works really well with the soup. For a plant-based/vegan version, use mushrooms, cannellini beans, or small florets of cauliflower instead of chicken. For a grain-free version, cauliflower rice would be excellent.

Cooking Times for Pressure Cooker: 3 minutes on Sauté + 20 minutes on Pressure Cook + 3 minutes more for pressure cooking, for the various steps

Yield: Serves 4

Ingredients:

1 tablespoon (15 ml) avocado oil

1 medium onion, diced

4–5 medium carrots, diced

¼–½ teaspoon ground turmeric

1 clove garlic, peeled

1 bunch fresh cilantro

1–2 limes

1 pound (454 g) boneless chicken thighs or breasts

1 quart (1 L) bone broth (home-made, page 149, or store-bought)

½ teaspoon onion powder

½ teaspoon garlic powder

1 teaspoon ground cumin

Dash of cayenne pepper

½ teaspoon dried thyme

Sea salt and black pepper, to taste

1 cup (180 g) uncooked quinoa

1 cup (165 g) frozen peas

About 5 Yukon gold potatoes, diced

1 can (4 ounces, or 113 g) green chiles or 1 mild- to medium-heat chile pepper, roasted

1. In a pressure cooker using the sauté setting, heat the oil. Add the onions and carrots, and sauté until fragrant. Add the turmeric, and sauté for about 1 minute.

2. In a food processor or blender, blend up the garlic and all the stems and some tops of the cilantro (reserving the rest for later), plus the zest and juice of a lime or two. Blend until it's a liquid; this is sometimes called a sofrito. Add this to the sautéed vegetables, and let it warm through.

3. Turn off sauté. Add the chicken, broth, and seasonings. Set to regular pressure for 20 minutes.

4. Release the pressure, remove the chicken, and shred the meat. Return the chicken to the pot.

5. Add the quinoa, some more cilantro leaves, the frozen peas, potatoes, and green chiles. Fill to the max fill line with water; water should cover everything by a couple of inches (5 cm) or so. Seal the pot and set to regular pressure for 3 minutes.

continued on following page

warming soups and stews

For Serving:

Sliced avocado

Fresh cilantro leaves

Lime wedges

Hot sauce

Aji Verde Sauce (recipe follows)

6. Release the pressure. Taste, and adjust the seasoning if needed. Spoon the soup into individual bowls. Top with avocado and more cilantro. Serve with plenty of lime wedges and some hot sauce on the side.

Note: *If you want to cook this on the stovetop, follow the same steps to get all the ingredients into the pot. Bring it to a boil over high heat, stirring occasionally, then reduce the heat to a simmer. Simmer for 20 to 30 minutes, stirring occasionally until the chicken is done. Remove the chicken, cut, and return it to the pot. Stir and serve.*

Aji Verde Sauce

My favorite way to serve it is to pour this into a gravy boat to pour over the top of the Aquadito de Pollo to your liking. This is so delicious you won't want to skip this part. You can thank me later!

Aji amarillo paste comes in a jar as a prepared sauce, and it is available at most stores. If you can't find this, use one small seeded and ribbed habanero pepper and some orange bell pepper to cut down on the heat slightly.

Yield: Serves 4

Ingredients:

2 cups (32 g) fresh cilantro

2 tablespoons (30 ml) fresh mint (about 15 leaves)

1 clove garlic

1 jalapeño, seeded and ribbed

½ cup (118 ml) mayonnaise (store-bought or homemade, page 69)

⅓ cup (40 g) crumbled Cotija cheese

2 tablespoons (30 ml) aji amarillo paste

1 lime

¼ teaspoon sea salt

¼ cup (59 ml) water

1. In a blender, add all the ingredients. Blend until it becomes a thick and creamy sauce.

Chapter 5

Lighter Plates

Spaghetti Squash Bake with Roasted Tomato Marinara

With so many people now diagnosed as celiac or choosing to go gluten-free for other reasons, it's easier to find great gluten-free pasta than it was years ago. However, I have been eating that way for so long that I remember the days when most of the gluten-free pastas were terrible—so all I was eating was spaghetti squash and zoodles! What I learned through my years of eating all sorts of substitutes is that there are times I want a bowl of pasta, yet there's a time and place for spaghetti squash.

For me, spaghetti squash is not an alternative to noodles anymore. Instead, I love using it in a recipe like this where it brings a softer-than-pasta texture and a bit more flavor to the dish (as well as nutrition). While you could use a store-bought sauce over spaghetti squash, roasting the tomatoes gives this homemade version a sweet and hearty flavor; it deepens the sauce and adds complexity. I think it holds its own with any of the top-tier store-bought sauces—and currently you do have to buy the expensive ones if you want to avoid junk oils, sugar, and citric acid!

Yield: Serves 4

Ingredients for the Marinara:

About 6 cups (1.1 kg) fresh grape or cherry tomatoes
¼ cup (59 ml) extra-virgin olive oil
7–8 cloves garlic
1 medium yellow onion, chopped
Pinch of crushed red pepper
Sea salt and black pepper, to taste
10–15 leaves fresh basil

Make the Marinara:

1. Preheat the oven to 400°F (200°C).

2. In a Dutch oven or other dish that can go from oven to stovetop, add all the ingredients except the basil. Roast for 30 minutes.

3. Transfer the dish to the stovetop over medium heat. Add the fresh basil, and bring to a simmer. Cook for 30 to 60 minutes.

4. Remove from the heat. Using an immersion blender, blend the sauce until smooth. Alternatively, you can transfer to a blender.

continued on following page

Ingredients for the Spaghetti Squash:

1 (3-pound [1.4-kg]) spaghetti squash

1 cup (237 ml) water (if using a pressure cooker)

Ingredients for the Cheese Layer:

1 cup (237 ml) ricotta or blended cottage cheese

½ cup (83 g) raw Cheddar cheese, plus more for sprinkling on top

½ cup (90 g) grated Parmesan cheese

Make the Spaghetti Squash:

1. Cut the spaghetti squash in half width-wise; this gives longer "noodles." Scoop out the seeds and discard them.

2. To cook in a pressure cooker, add the cup of water, then place the cut squash on a trivet; it will be over the water. Pressure-cook for 3 minutes, then manual release the pressure.

3. If roasting, preheat the oven to 400°F (200°C), and line a baking sheet with parchment paper. Place the squash halves face down on the lined sheet, and roast them for 35 to 40 minutes.

4. Let them cool a bit before handling. Pull apart the spaghetti squash with a fork and place the "noodles" in a large mixing bowl. Drain any excess liquid.

Make the Cheese Layer:

1. In a mixing bowl, combine the cheeses.

Assemble the Squash Bake:

1. Preheat the oven to 350°F (175°C).

2. In an 8 × 6-inch (20 × 15-cm), or similar size, broil-safe baking dish, build in layers as you would a lasagna. Add one-third of the spaghetti squash, then one-quarter of the sauce, then one-third of the cheese mixture.

3. Repeat, making three layers total. Top with the sauce, then sprinkle with the cheese.

4. Bake for 30 minutes. Turn the oven to broil. Broil for 5 minutes until the cheese begins to brown, keeping a close watch.

5. Remove from the oven. Let cool for 10 minutes before serving.

How to Store: *The marinara can be stored for up to 1 week in the fridge or 1 month in the freezer.*

Falafel Night with Quinoa Tabouli and Tzatziki

Falafel mix and premade falafel balls are tempting, but you never quite know what you're going to get. If you shop around, you might get lucky, but many are loaded up with preservatives or stabilizers—and even the best may contain inflammatory oils. Making your own falafel removes questionable ingredients and the flavor is so much better, too; falafel should be bright and fresh!

At my house we do make this into a whole weekend-night endeavor—because it feels special, and also because it's more involved than many of the other recipes in this book. But we all pitch in and have fun with it around here! If you have kids who can help, get an older child making the tzatziki. A younger child will likely be fascinated by the food processor.

Keep in mind that the falafel dough and tzatziki need to be made ahead of time. The falafel dough should be stored in an airtight container for at least 1 hour before cooking and up to overnight is great. Store the tzatziki in an airtight container in the refrigerator for at least 2 hours before serving and up to 3 days.

Yield: Serves 4

Ingredients for the Falafel:

3 cups (525 g) dried chickpeas, soaked overnight in water and a splash of apple cider vinegar, drained, and rinsed

1 medium shallot or small onion, diced

Handful of fresh flat-leaf parsley

3–5 cloves garlic, raw or roasted

1½ tablespoons (12 g) gluten-free flour (I used garbanzo bean flour, if available. Otherwise Bob's Red Mill 1:1 gluten-free blend.)

1½ teaspoons sea salt, or to taste

2 teaspoons (5 g) ground cumin

¼ teaspoon cayenne pepper

Pinch of ground cardamom

½ teaspoon black pepper, or to taste

Avocado oil, for frying

Make the Falafel:

1. To the bowl of a food processor, add all the ingredients.

2. Pulse and process until you get a coarse dough. (You're not going for hummus, but you also don't want it so chunky it won't hold together.) Scoop out a little and see if it holds together a bit; if not, pulse a little more and test again. Transfer to a bowl, cover tightly, and store in the fridge for 1 to 2 hours.

3. Line a plate with a paper towel or a tea towel. In a 10-inch (25-cm) skillet over medium heat, add ½ inch (1.3 cm) or so of avocado oil and heat it until it is nice and hot. Using an ice cream scoop (I use my

continued on following page

Ingredients for the Tzatziki:

¾ of a large seedless cucumber

2 cups (453 g) plain full-fat Greek or regular yogurt

2–4 cloves garlic, pressed

1 teaspoon finely chopped fresh dill

1 teaspoon apple cider vinegar or another light vinegar

½ teaspoon sea salt

1 teaspoon good olive oil

Optional: ¼ teaspoon white pepper

Ingredients for the Quinoa Tabouli:

2 cups (360 g) sprouted quinoa

1¾ cups (296 ml) water

¼ cup (59 ml) extra-virgin olive oil

Zest and juice of 1 lemon

2 teaspoons (9 g) sea salt

½ teaspoon black pepper

1 medium shallot, finely diced

1 tablespoon (15 ml) apple cider vinegar

3 cups (162 g) finely chopped fresh flat-leaf parsley

3 cups (162 g) finely chopped arugula

½ cup (27 g) loosely packed fresh mint leaves, finely chopped

2 cups (400 g) diced grape or cherry tomatoes

1 large Persian cucumber, finely chopped

#24) or a spoon, form the chickpea mixture into balls and carefully place them in the oil, one ball of falafel at a time, making sure not to place them too close to each other or overcrowd the pan.

4. Cook the falafel on each side for 3 to 4 minutes until they are golden and crisp outside.

5. Using a slotted spoon or spider strainer, remove to the lined plate.

Make the Tzatziki:

1. Place the cucumber on a flour-sack or tea towel on top of your cutting board. Shred, add a good pinch of salt, toss, and let sit for a minute. Then gather up the towel and squeeze out the liquid over a small bowl. (You can reserve the liquid for a cucumber electrolyte water or use in a salad dressing.)

2. Place the drained cucumber in a large bowl. Add the remaining ingredients. Mix gently to combine.

3. Cover and refrigerate for 2 hours or up to a couple days.

Make the Quinoa Tabouli:

1. In a small saucepan with a lid, combine the sprouted quinoa with the water. Bring to a boil, then lower the heat to a simmer and cook, covered, for 12 to 14 minutes. Allow the quinoa to cool. (You can make this the night before and refrigerate.)

2. In a large bowl, mix the remaining ingredients. Add the cooled quinoa, and mix to combine.

How to Serve:

In a large, shallow bowl or platter, place the falafel, quinoa tabouli, and tzatziki side by side.

Top-Notch Ramen

When my husband and I first got married, we thought we were really elevating our tiny budget dinners by adding veggies to our ramen nights. I think back on those nights fondly and so, after going gluten-free, I missed our modified ramen. While I eventually found a gluten-free ramen noodle I liked, the harder part was replacing those weird seasoning packets filled with ingredients like MSG, natural flavors, wheat flour, TBHQ, and of course, a ton of sodium. (I found even higher cost, more "natural" versions have things like natural and artificial flavors, corn oil, disodium inosinate . . . and some still use MSG.) I clearly had to make my own broth. Through trial and error, I hit upon the recipe below. So, choose your own noodles, and play with the toppings on this one. But make sure to try my top-notch ramen broth!

Yield: Serves 4

Ingredients:

1 tablespoon (15 ml) avocado oil

½ cup (45 g) shredded carrot

1 stalk celery, sliced

1 medium shallot, minced

1–2 cloves garlic, pressed

½-inch (1.3-cm) piece fresh
  ginger, grated

2 cups (480 ml) Bone Broth
  (page 149)

½ teaspoon fish sauce

2–3 tablespoons (30–45 ml)
  coconut aminos

½ cup (82 g) frozen peas

⅛ teaspoon ground mustard

⅛ teaspoon garlic powder

Dash of cayenne pepper, or to taste

Sea salt and black pepper, to taste

1 block (70 g) rice ramen noodles
  (I like Lotus Foods brand.)

For Serving:

Sliced scallions

1. In a medium saucepan over medium heat, heat the avocado oil. Add the carrots, celery, shallots, garlic, and ginger. Sauté for 3 to 5 minutes until tender and fragrant.

2. Add the remaining ingredients, and bring to a boil. Lower the heat, and simmer for about 4 minutes until the noodles are tender.

3. Top with scallions and serve.

Note: *Other fun toppings include a halved soft-boiled egg, cilantro leaves, chili oil, toasted sesame seeds, nori, kimchi, and slices of chicken, beef, or pork. Serve with plenty of hot sauce on the side.*

Grain-Free Crispy Fish with Oven Fries and ALLT Coleslaw

I loved going to Chippies in England before I was gluten-free. So, this recipe is inspired by that, though now that I have kids, we more often make them as "fish sticks" instead of as fillets. No matter the size you choose, these have a nice crunch on the outside even when baked, and they remain flaky, buttery, and tender in the middle. Use them as the main on this plate with fries and slaw, or try them in fish tacos or burritos!

You might be tempted to buy bagged fries, but store-bought fries often have not the best oils and the best ones are not cheap. I worked on my method over time and am happy sharing these with anyone—even the most devoted fry fans. I love coleslaw as well, and to me this plate just isn't complete without it. Homemade is just so fresh and crisp, which makes me enjoy its creaminess so much more.

Yield: Serves 4

Ingredients:

1½ pounds (680 g) wild mahi-mahi fillets or wild Atlantic cod

1 cup (120 g) tapioca flour

2 teaspoons (99 g) sea salt, divided, plus more to taste

¼ teaspoon black pepper, divided, plus more to taste

2 large eggs

1 cup (100 g) almond flour or coconut flour

1 teaspoon garlic powder

1 teaspoon paprika

Optional: avocado oil, for frying

For Serving:

Homemade Tartar Sauce (recipe follows)

ALLT Coleslaw (recipe follows)

Oven Fries (recipe follows)

1. Cut the fish into sticks about 1 inch (2.5 cm) across and a few inches long. Pat dry with a clean cloth or paper towel, and set them aside.

2. Prepare your breading station: In one dish, combine the tapioca flour with 1 teaspoon salt and ⅛ teaspoon pepper. In a second dish, thoroughly mix the eggs with a pinch of salt and pepper. In a third dish, mix the flour with the garlic powder, paprika, and 1 teaspoon salt and ⅛ teaspoon pepper. Have a wire rack ready.

3. Dip each piece of fish into the tapioca. Shake off the excess. Dip it in the egg, then the flour. Place it on the wire rack to rest while the oil is heating up.

4. To Fry: In a stainless pan, heat the oil over medium heat. Carefully add a few fish sticks at a time. Cook each side until crispy, a couple minutes per side. (Fish cooks fast.) Place on the wire rack while you finish the rest.

continued on following page

Tip: *If you prefer more of a fish-and-chips vibe, leave the fillets whole or cut them into larger, more rustic pieces.*

To Bake: Preheat the oven to 400°F (200°C). Place the fish sticks on a parchment paper–lined baking sheet, and lightly spray them with olive oil or avocado oil. Bake for 15 to 20 minutes, or until the internal temperature is 145°F (63°C).

Homemade Tartar Sauce

Yield: Serves 4

Ingredients:

1 teaspoon honey

1 teaspoon grainy mustard

½ cup (104 g) mayonnaise (store-bought or homemade, page 69)

3 tablespoons (44 ml) finely chopped fermented pickles or fermented pickle relish

1 tablespoon (15 ml) fresh lemon juice

Sea salt and black pepper, to taste

1. Mix all the ingredients together to combine.

2. Serve with the fish sticks for dipping and deliciousness.

ALLT Coleslaw

Yield: Serves 4

Ingredients for the Dressing:

1¼ cups (260 g) mayonnaise (store-bought or homemade, page 69)

½ cup (96 g) coconut sugar

½ cup (118 ml) apple cider vinegar

¼ teaspoon celery seed

Salt, to taste

Ingredients for the Slaw:

2 medium carrots, shredded

½ head purple cabbage, shredded

1 medium green cabbage, shredded

Make the Dressing:

1. In a large bowl, whisk together all the dressing ingredients. Taste and adjust the seasonings if needed.

Make the Slaw:

1. Add the veggies, and mix to combine. Taste and adjust the seasoning if needed.

2. Store in the refrigerator until ready to serve.

How to Store: *You can make this a day in advance if needed. It keeps for several days in the fridge.*

Oven Fries

Potatoes are part of the Dirty Dozen, and they should be eaten organic whenever possible. On top of that, most fries at restaurants are cooked in oils high in omega-6 fatty acids and are toxic to our bodies and are not a great choice. Do I eat fries out? Heck yeah. But I always feel gross after, and have been getting them less and less.

Yield: Serves 4

Ingredients:

3 pounds (1.4 kg, 3 to 4 medium) russet potatoes, peeled if desired

¼ cup (59 ml) avocado oil

Salt, to taste

Optional:

Seasonings of choice

1. Cut the potatoes into sticks about ½-inch (1.3-cm) wide.

2. Put the sticks in a big bowl of cold water and let them sit for 30 minutes, or refrigerate them up to overnight.

3. Preheat the oven to 400°F (200°C). Line baking sheets with parchment paper. Drain and pat dry the potato with a clean cloth.

4. In a large bowl, mix the avocado oil with salt and seasonings, if using. Toss the potatoes in the seasoned oil and spread them out in a single layer on the lined sheets. (They get crispier if they have a little space around them, so don't overcrowd the pan.)

5. Bake for 35 to 45 minutes until golden and crispy. Turn the oven to broil for the last 5 minutes or so to toast the tops. Keep a close eye, though!

Tip: *If the potatoes will sit in the water for longer than 30 minutes, store them in the fridge until you're ready. This will keep the potatoes from turning black, and it will also help draw out some starch so that you end up with a crispier fry.*

lighter plates

Seared Scallops with Pesto Pasta

Scallops are so expensive to order out, but they are so tasty. Would you believe it if I told you they are even better at home? With just a little practice, I've found there's nothing like a scallop fresh out of the pan. The pesto in this recipe is very traditional, bright and herby with a salty, rich cheese. For the pesto you can also use other nuts such as walnuts (though we don't as my husband is allergic, so we tend to use cashews as a substitute). Macadamia nuts would be excellent in this recipe with the scallops.

Yield: Serves 4

Ingredients for the Pesto Pasta:

2–4 cloves garlic

⅓ cup (45 g) pine nuts

5 cups (384 g) fresh basil leaves, loosely packed

1 cup (59 ml) extra-virgin olive oil

1 cup (100 g) freshly grated Parmesan cheese, plus more for serving

1 teaspoon sea salt

1 box (12 ounces, or 340 g) gluten-free farfalle pasta

Make the Pesto:

1. In a food processor, pulse the garlic and pine nuts until finely chopped. Add the basil, and process for about 30 seconds.

2. While the motor is running, drizzle in the oil. Continue to process until it becomes thoroughly pureed.

3. Add the Parmesan and salt. Process until fully incorporated and becomes the texture you like.

4. Cook the pasta according to the package directions. Drain it well and top it with the pesto sauce.

Scallops

Scallops don't just taste great—they are an excellent source of vitamin B$_{12}$ and phosphorus. They are also a good source of protein, selenium, choline, zinc, magnesium, and potassium. This is brain food! They're not all created equal though. Quality matters. Wild-caught is a better choice than farmed as a rule. Flash frozen is a good thing.

Ingredients for the Scallops:

1–1½ pounds (454–680 g) wild scallops

Sea salt and black pepper, to taste

About 3 tablespoons (85 g) salted butter, divided

About 3 tablespoons (44 ml) extra-virgin olive oil, divided

Make the Scallops:

1. Heat a flat-bottomed skillet over medium heat. Pat the scallops dry with a paper towel or a clean cloth, and season them with salt and pepper.

2. Add 1 tablespoon (14 g) butter and 1 tablespoon (15 ml) oil to your hot pan. When melted, add the scallops, leaving plenty of room so they don't steam—you want a nice sear on them. Leave them untouched for 3 to 4 minutes, flip, and cook the other side until golden, about 2 minutes.

3. Repeat until all the scallops are cooked, adding more butter and oil as needed. Serve the scallops on top of the pesto pasta with freshly grated Parmesan.

How to Store: *Cover the pesto with a thin layer of extra-virgin olive oil to prevent oxidation. Refrigerate for up to 1 week. To freeze, scoop into ice cube trays or silicone molds, freeze until solid, then move to airtight storage. Freeze for up to 3 months.*

Simple Salmon Patties

When you buy premade patties of any type, but especially fish or more expensive proteins, you have to watch out for fillers, vegetable oils, coloring, and preservatives. Usually it's a lot of questionable ingredients for something that should be a five-ish ingredient recipe! The other nice thing is that when you make these yourself, you can make sure you're using great-tasting wild salmon

Yield: Serves 4

Ingredients:

2 large eggs, lightly beaten

Juice of 1 lemon

Sea salt and black pepper, to taste

¼ teaspoon garlic powder

2 cans (5 ounces, or 142 g) wild salmon, drained

About ¼ cup (30 g) coconut or almond flour

For Pan-Frying: 2 tablespoons (30 ml) avocado oil

Optional, for Serving:

Buns or a salad

Vegetable of choice

Rice or pasta

1. In a large bowl, mix all the ingredients. You want a nice moldable consistency, so if needed, add more flour, a little at a time.

2. You can use a 2-inch (5-cm) ice cream scoop to form the mixture into six patties, or size them any way you like.

3. To Fry: In a 10-inch (25-cm) skillet, heat the avocado oil over medium heat. Add the salmon burgers. Cook them for 5 to 8 minutes, flipping about halfway through until both sides are nice and golden.

   To Bake: Preheat the oven to 400°F (200°C). Line a baking sheet with parchment paper. Place the patties on the lined sheet. Bake them for about 20 minutes, depending on patty size.

4. Serve the patties on buns or a salad, or offer them as the main dish alongside a vegetable and rice or pasta.

Pineapple Chicken Curry

Pineapple cores are high in bromelain, great anti-inflammatory agents, digestive enzymes, and antiparasitics. Cores are tough and not very edible, but save them, freeze them, and use them like vegetable scraps in a stock, stew, or curry. While curry has some heat, with the coconut milk, pineapple, and all the veggies, my kids (who are both a little spice-sensitive) didn't mind the spice at all. Adjust as needed if you have low spice tolerance.

Yield: Serves 4

Ingredients:

1½–2½ teaspoons (5–10 ml) coconut oil, divided

1½ pounds (680 g) boneless skinless chicken thighs

1 medium onion, diced

⅛ to ¼ teaspoon ground turmeric

1 jar (12½ ounces, or 354 g) red madras curry sauce of choice. (I use Maya Kaimal; they come in varying heat levels, so start light and you can always add more if desired.)

2 cloves garlic, pressed

1–4 pineapple cores

⅔–1 whole medium pineapple, cut into chunks

1 medium red bell pepper, sliced

1 pound (454 g) broccoli crowns, stalks shredded or minced, and florets chopped small

2 medium carrots, shredded

Handful of fresh cilantro

½ teaspoon sea salt

1 can (13½ ounces, or 383 g) full-fat coconut milk

2–3 cups (226–339 g) mung bean sprouts

For Serving:

Rice or cauliflower rice

Sliced scallions

Fresh cilantro

Lime wedges

Sriracha-style hot sauce

1. In a 10-inch (25-cm) skillet, heat 1 to 2 teaspoons of coconut oil over medium heat. Add the chicken thighs, and sear until the skin is brown and crispy. Remove and set them aside.

2. Add the onions, and sauté for about 5 minutes until translucent and tender. Create a well in the center of the pan, and add another ½ teaspoon of coconut oil and the turmeric. Toast it for 1 to 2 minutes, then stir.

3. Add the curry, and toast it for 1 to 2 minutes, then stir. Add the garlic, and sauté for 1 to 2 minutes.

4. Add the pineapple, vegetables, cilantro, and salt. Pour in the coconut milk, bring to a boil, and reduce to a simmer. Cook for about 20 minutes, then add the chicken back in. Cook for about 10 minutes, or until all the ingredients are tender. Remove from the heat.

5. Carefully remove and discard the pineapple cores. Add the mung bean sprouts, and stir to combine.

6. Serve in a shallow bowl with rice in the middle. Top with fresh scallions and cilantro. Serve with lime wedges and hot sauce.

lighter plates

Thai Lettuce Cups with Peanut Sauce

This used to be a family favorite to order out at a certain chain restaurant. For maximum fun, you have to serve it family style so everyone can build their own little cups. The peanut sauce is optional, but it packs a big flavor punch. It has a gingery bite, is sweet, and is packed with umami. (It's the base of the dressing for the Fresh Thai-Style Salad on page 81; if you try it and like it!) What's more, it's full of prebiotics and fiber for gut love and so much nourishment. Pile up the goodies. Have fun.

Yield: Serves 4

Ingredients:

1–2 teaspoons (15–30 ml) coconut oil

1 pound (454 g) pasture-raised ground lamb or other protein of choice

Juice of 1 lime

3 tablespoons (44 ml) coconut aminos

2 teaspoons (4 g) freshly grated ginger

1 teaspoon fish sauce

3–5 cloves garlic, pressed

1 teaspoon sriracha

2 tablespoons (30 ml) coconut sugar

For Serving:

Bibb, butter, iceberg or whatever lettuce you have that can be used as a little cup

Peanut Sauce (recipe follows)

Lime wedges

Sriracha

Optional Toppings:

Julienned bell pepper

Shredded carrot

Chopped scallions

Fresh cilantro

Minced shallot

Thinly sliced purple cabbage

Chopped nuts or crunchy seeds

1. In a 10-inch (25-cm) skillet, heat the coconut oil over medium heat. Add the ground lamb. Sauté until cooked through, 6 to 7 minutes.

2. In a small pan, whisk together the remaining ingredients. Cook over medium-low heat until the sauce thickens.

3. Pour over your protein, and stir gently to combine.

4. Spoon the mixture into the lettuce cups, adding a dollop of peanut sauce on each. Serve with extra sauce on the side, as well as any toppings you like.

Tip: *You can also make this in a slow cooker for 4 hours on high or 6 hours on low, or in an Instant Pot for 6 minutes.*

Peanut Sauce

I toss all this in the blender. An immersion blender, food processor, or whisk all work great too. Any nut butter or sun butter is great. Use what you have and like.

Yield: Makes about ¾ cup; serves 4+

Ingredients:

½ cup (128 g) peanut butter or cashew butter

Juice of half a lime

1 teaspoon sriracha

1- to 2-inch (2.5- to 5-cm) knob fresh ginger, grated (about 2 teaspoons)

1 clove garlic, pressed

1 tablespoon (15 ml) honey

2 tablespoons (30 ml) coconut aminos

1 tablespoon (15 ml) water or more to reach desired consistency

Salt, to taste

1. In a blender, add all the sauce ingredients. Blend until smooth.

Chapter 6

Heartier Dishes

Chicken Potpie

One of my best friends, Amy, who now works with me and is my right hand, lives very similar to the way I do. She shared the base of this recipe many years ago, and over the years it has evolved a bit for both of us. It's optional, but my vote is always double the crust! Make enough for top and bottom. The crust gets a nice crunch on top, but it still has a satisfying dough feel. It's the perfect contrast to the hearty, soupy filling. It gives you the nostalgic vibes you want in a potpie. The crust is the hard part, but it's worth it. The rest is easy mode.

Yield: Serves 4

Ingredients for the Crust:

1 cup (100 g) blanched almond flour

¼ cup (30 g) tapioca flour

½ teaspoon paprika

½ teaspoon sea salt

¼ teaspoon baking powder

⅛ teaspoon black pepper

¼ cup (57 g) cold salted butter, cut into small pieces

1 large egg

3 tablespoons (44 ml) cold water

Make the Crust:

1. In a food processor, add all the dry ingredients. Process until combined. Add the butter, egg, and water. Pulse until mixed and a dough forms.

2. Scoop out the dough, and place it on a piece of parchment paper. Store it in the freezer for 30 minutes.

3. Place the chilled dough between two sheets of parchment paper. Roll out the dough to the size and shape of your pan (I use a 9 × 13-inch [23 × 33-cm]), using your pan as a mold or stencil.

4. Store the crust in the freezer until ready to use.

continued on following page

heartier dishes

Ingredients for the Filling:

2 tablespoons (28 g) salted butter

1 medium yellow onion, diced

3–4 medium carrots, diced

3–4 stalks celery, diced

1 pound (454 g) or more precooked chicken, diced

2 cups (330 g) frozen peas

1 cup (113 g) frozen green beans

1 teaspoon dried thyme

½ teaspoon paprika

¼ teaspoon ground mustard

¼ teaspoon ground coriander

⅛ teaspoon chili powder

¾ teaspoon granulated garlic

¼ teaspoon onion powder

Sea salt and black pepper, to taste

1 cup (237 ml) chicken broth or Bone Broth (page 149)

1 tablespoon (8 g) tapioca flour

Make the Filling:

1. In a 10-inch (25-cm) skillet, cook the chicken and set aside. Using the same pan, melt the butter. Add the onions, carrots, and celery, and sauté for about 5 minutes until tender.

2. Add the chicken, frozen veggies, and seasonings. Cook, stirring occasionally, until the veggies are thawed and soften.

3. Add the broth. Make a well in the middle of the pan, then whisk in the tapioca flour. Stir to combine. It should become a nice, thick gravy consistency.

Make the Potpie:

1. Preheat the oven to 350°F (175°C).

2. Spoon the filling into the pan. Place the piece of dough on top; unlike some pot pies, setting the dough on top is enough here, and there is no need to pinch around the edges to seal. Make three slots on the top to vent.

3. Bake for 40 minutes. If you would like to toast the crust, place it under the broiler for the last couple minutes. But keep a close eye to make sure it doesn't burn.

4. Let it rest for 10 minutes before cutting and serving to give it time to set back up and hold together.

Note: *This potpie is even more delicious with a bottom crust as well! Simply double the dough ingredients, and split it into two pieces before rolling it out and placing it in the freezer. Use some ghee, butter, or avocado oil to grease the pan before laying one piece of the dough in the bottom.*

Turkey Burger Bowls with Sweet Potato Cubies and Pickled Red Onions

This is an easy weeknight meal, a burger in a bite with some fun flavor pops. The cubies are simple, but they feel more special and fun than normal oven fries. They get a nice crust with a soft, tender middle. Experiment with seasonings on them too. Different seasoned salts or spice blends can take this bowl in whole new directions. I often use a seasoned salt blend or make up my own with ingredients like garlic, onion, mustard, paprika, salt, and pepper. Don't worry about not having time for the pickled onions: They are quick-pickled and not a long ferment.

Yield: Serves 4

Ingredients for the Turkey Burger:

2 tablespoons (30 ml) olive oil, divided

1 small yellow onion, finely minced

1–2 cloves garlic, pressed

1½ pounds (680 g) ground turkey

1 teaspoon sea salt

¼ teaspoon black pepper

Optional:

Cheese slices of choice, extra seasoning options

Ingredients for the Bowl:

Chopped lettuce

Chopped tomato

Sliced avocado

Sliced pickles

Sweet Potato Cubies (recipe follows)

Pickled Red Onions (recipe follows)

Make the Turkey Burger:

1. In a 10-inch (25-cm) skillet, heat 1 tablespoon (15 ml) oil over medium heat. Add the onions, and sauté them until almost tender, about 4 minutes. Add the garlic, and sauté for about 1 minute. Set it aside to cool a little.

2. In a medium bowl, combine the cooked onions and garlic with the ground turkey. Add the salt and pepper, then gently mix. Form the mixture into six patties.

3. In the same pan where you cooked the onions, heat the remaining 1 tablespoon (15 ml) of oil over medium heat. Add the patties, and cook for 3 to 4 minutes per side (depending on the size of your patties) until the internal temperature is 165°F (74°C). If desired, top each burger with a slice of cheese during the last 2 minutes of cooking.

Make the Bowl:

1. Serve the burgers over a bed of your favorite lettuce, alongside tomatoes, avocado, pickles, sweet potato cubies, and some pickled red onions.

continued on following page

heartier dishes

Sweet Potato Cubies

Sweet and savory, with a bit of a crisp on the edges, and a soft, fluffy center. These cubes of goodness are a breeze to whip up and are a perfect accompaniment to many dishes, especially these turkey burger bowls.

Yield: Serves 4

Ingredients:

3–4 medium sweet potatoes

2 tablespoons (30 ml) fat, such as duck fat, bacon fat, olive oil, or avocado oil

⅛ teaspoon onion powder

⅛ teaspoon garlic powder

⅛ teaspoon paprika

Sea salt and black pepper, to taste

Tip: *Instead of individual seasonings, you can use your favorite seasoning salt.*

1. Preheat the oven to 400°F (200°C). Peel the sweet potatoes and dice them into ½-inch (1.3-cm) cubes. In a large bowl, toss the potato cubes with the fat. Add the seasonings, and toss to combine.

2. Heat a cast-iron skillet (or other oven-safe skillet) over medium-high heat. Add the potatoes. Cook on the stovetop, without moving the potatoes, for about 5 minutes until one side of the potatoes starts getting a little crisp.

3. Flip the potato cubes and move the pan to the oven. Bake for 30 to 35 minutes until the potatoes are fork-tender.

Pickled Red Onions

After my first try at a quick pickled red onion, they became a staple. They are so easy and great with many dishes!

Yield: Serves 4

Ingredients:

2 medium red onions, halved and thinly sliced

¼ cup (59 ml) fresh lime juice

½ cup (118 ml) apple cider vinegar

¼ cup (59 ml) honey

1 teaspoon sea salt

Pinch of crushed red pepper

1. Heat up water in a kettle or a pot to boiling. Place the onions in a large bowl, then pour over the boiling water. Let sit for 10 seconds. Drain off the water.

2. In a small pot, combine the lime juice, vinegar, honey, salt, and crushed red pepper. Place over medium heat and cook, stirring, until the honey is dissolved.

3. Pour over the onions, then toss gently to cover. Transfer to the fridge, and allow the onions to cool before serving.

How to Store: *The pickled onions will keep in the refrigerator for up to 2 weeks—if they last that long!*

The Wholesome Whole Chicken

If your family is "addicted" to store-bought rotisserie chicken, this recipe is your swap. While you don't get the golden skin, thanks to the seasonings in my Master Blend (and maybe a few herbs if you're feeling fancy), there's still big flavor. Eat it as-is with sweet potatoes or rice, or add the chicken meat to pasta, soups, chicken salad, or Chicken Potpie (page 141). And, of course, use it in Enchiladas Verdes (page 150), Mediterranean-Style Pasta Salad (page 77), or White Bean Chicken Chili (page 105).

Yield: Serves 4+

Cooking Times:

Pressure cooker: 35 minutes

Oven: 15 minutes at 425°F (220°C), then 45 to 60 minutes at 250°F (120°C) until internal temperature reaches 165°F (74°C)

Slow cooker: High for 3 to 4 hours or low for 4 to 6 hours until internal temperature reaches 165°F (74°C)

Ingredients:

1 cup (237 ml) water

1 (4–5-pound [1.8–2.3-kg]) whole chicken, innards and giblets removed, patted dry with a paper towel

Sea salt, to taste (Omit this if your seasoning blend includes salt.)

Master Blend Seasoning (page 148) or seasoning of choice, to taste

Tip: *Depending on how I use the chicken, I can get up to three dinners from one bird. I freeze some of the meat to be used at a later time. And the carcass will make 2+ quarts (2 L) of bone broth.*

1. First, make sure your pressure cooker is big enough to fit your bird! I find a 6-quart (1-L) cooker will fit a 5-pound (2.3-kg) chicken. Then add the steam rack in the bottom, and pour in the water.

2. Generously sprinkle the salt and seasoning mix on both sides of the chicken, using your hands to rub it evenly onto the skin. Then sprinkle the salt and seasoning inside the cavity of the chicken. Spread it around to coat evenly. Place the chicken on the rack in the pressure cooker.

3. Pop the lid on the pressure cooker and lock it. Set the vent to "seal." Press the "poultry" button if your pressure cooker has one, or set to 30 minutes at regular pressure.

4. Once ready, remove your perfectly cooked and delicious chicken. Transfer it to a cutting board, and let it rest for 5 minutes before carving.

How to Store: *You can store the chicken whole or remove the meat first (which is easier to do when warm). I keep my carcass for making Bone Broth (page 149). When placed in an airtight container, the chicken will last for 3 to 4 days in the fridge or up to 6 months in the freezer.*

continued on following page

heartier dishes

Master Blend

This is my go-to spice recipe. Feel free to adjust salt ratios to your own tastes/needs/preferences.

Yield: Fills regular-size spice jar (about 3.6–4 ounces)

Ingredients:

4 teaspoons (12 g) salt
2 tablespoons (16 g) garlic powder
2 tablespoons (16 g) onion powder
4 teaspoons (12 g) ground mustard
2 teaspoons coriander
4 teaspoons (12 g) paprika
2 teaspoons black pepper
¼ teaspoon cayenne

1. Mix all ingredients together. Add to spice jar and use on any desired recipe!

Taco Seasoning Blend

Other than my Master Blend, this is the premade seasoning I turn to most. I use taco seasoning all the time, but nearly every store-bought taco seasoning has ingredients I'd personally rather not ingest: silicon dioxide, artificial flavors, undisclosed "spices," MSG, inflammatory oils, "natural flavors" that can include all sorts of natural and disgusting stuff, maltodextrin, and more. Yep, it's time to start making your own taco seasoning! I make a triple batch or so each time so I have the blend on hand any time I need it. As written, this mix balances smoky, spicy, savory, salty, and sweet just to my liking. But of course, give it a try and adjust it for your family's taste.

Yield: Makes about ¼ cup

Ingredients:

¼ teaspoon cayenne pepper
¼ teaspoon black pepper
1 teaspoon sea salt
1 teaspoon garlic granules or powder
1 teaspoon onion powder
1 teaspoon ground cumin
1 teaspoon dried oregano
1 teaspoon paprika
1 teaspoon coconut sugar
2 teaspoons (6 g) chili powder
2 teaspoons (6 g) chipotle chili powder (If you don't have this, just use regular chili powder.)

1. Mix all the ingredients in a 2-cup (473-ml) or larger bowl with a spoon or whisk. Store in an airtight container.

Bone Broth

Bone broth has a host of benefits, and its rise in popularity over the past decade means you can now buy it prepackaged. But should you? Bone broth is easy to make, costs pennies, and I believe that the better the animal was cared for, the better the broth and its benefits. If you use more water, you will have a more diluted broth that will not be gelatinous. If you want an even thicker and more gelatinous broth, use more bones and consider adding chicken feet. Don't omit the splash of apple cider vinegar, which helps pull minerals from the bones. You can add seasonings and veggies if you want to, but I prefer leaving them out to keep the broth both simple and versatile. (See it used in recipes on page 156 and 159!)

Yield: Serves 4

Cooking Times:
Pressure cooker: 1 hour and
 30 minutes
Slow cooker: 24 to 48 hours
Stovetop: 24 to 48 hours

Ingredients:
1 (4–5 pound [1.8–2.3-kg]) whole chicken carcass (like from The Wholesome Whole Chicken, page 147), or similar amount of bones, as well as giblets, skin, cartilage, and any drippings
1½ quarts (1.4 L) water
2–3 tablespoons (30–44 ml) apple cider vinegar
1 teaspoon sea salt
½ teaspoon black peppercorns
2–3 bay leaves

Optional:
Vegetables (such as carrots, onion, celery, garlic)

1. Place all the ingredients in a pressure cooker, slow cooker, or large soup pot. Add enough water to come 1 inch (2.5 cm) above everything. Leave it to cook until it's reduced and concentrated; this can take 1 hour and 30 minutes (for pressure cooker) to 2 days (for slow cooker or stovetop).

Note: *When adding the water, it's okay to push the chicken down beneath the surface, and it's also fine if the water doesn't quite cover the chicken. I recommend sticking to the 1½ quarts (1.4 L) per chicken for the best broth.*

2. Set a fine-mesh strainer over a large bowl. Carefully pour broth over. Toss out the solids, and allow the broth to cool. The more concentrated the bone broth, the more gelatinous it will become as it cools.

3. Use as a soup base and in recipes calling for chicken broth. You can also pour it into a mug and sip—it is comforting and has several health benefits!

How to Store: *Store the bone broth in airtight containers, leaving room at the top for expansion (especially if using glass). The bone broth stays good in the fridge for about 1 week or in the freezer for up to 12 months.*

Enchiladas Verdes with Refried Beans and Taqueria-Style Roasted Carrots

These are classic enchiladas with a sauce that's so delicious and more wholesome than store-bought sauces. You will need fresh tomatillos though. If they aren't easy to find near you, when you do find them at the market, you can double or triple this recipe and freeze it. Actually, the same goes for the enchiladas! I love making a double or triple batch. I usually refrigerate them to eat the same week, but I have frozen these before and found they reheat well that way. This recipe calls for chicken, but you can fill the enchiladas with potatoes, or black beans, or lentils, or shredded beef, or whatever you want!

The refried beans are usually made from leftover pinto beans. You can make them as thin or thick as you want. The carrots are inspired by the pickled jalapeños and carrots you'll sometimes find in salsa bars at restaurants.

Yield: Serves 4

Ingredients for the Enchilada Sauce:

12–14 tomatillos

1 medium yellow onion or large shallot, quartered

5 cloves garlic, peeled

1 poblano chile, seeded, or 1 can (7 ounces, or 198 g) mild green chiles

Handful of fresh cilantro (stems are fine), chopped (about 1 cup [16 g])

Salt, to taste

½ cup (120 g) sour cream

Make the Enchilada Sauce:

1. Preheat the oven to 350°F (175°C).

2. Place the tomatillos, onions, garlic, and fresh chile, if using, on a baking sheet. Roast for 20 minutes until there are some brown spots and the vegetables are slightly blistered and tender.

3. Add everything to a blender or food processor. Process until well blended. Taste and adjust the seasoning if needed.

4. Pour the sauce into a medium saucepan over high heat. Bring it to a boil. Lower to a simmer and cook for 20 to 30 minutes to really marry and deepen the flavors. Near the end of cooking, stir in the sour cream to incorporate.

continued on following page

Ingredients for the Chicken:

1½ pounds (680 g) boneless, skinless chicken thighs

1 cup (237 ml) water

1 teaspoon seasonings of choice

Ingredients for the Enchiladas:

12–14 corn tortillas

Optional: raw Cheddar cheese for sprinkling

Garnishes: chopped tomatoes, sliced black olives, sliced jalapeños

For Serving:

Refried Beans (recipe follows)

Taqueria-Style Roasted Carrots (recipe follows)

Make the Chicken:

1. In an Instant Pot, add the chicken and the water, along with any seasonings. Cook for 6 minutes on high pressure.

2. Remove the chicken to a cutting board, and let it sit until it's cool enough to handle. Shred the meat using your hands, two forks, or a mixer (see note).

Make the Enchiladas:

1. Preheat the oven to 350°F (175°C). Spread a thin layer of the sauce in the bottom of a 9 × 13-inch (23 × 33-cm) pan.

2. Warm up the tortillas over the flames of a gas stove, or on a griddle.

3. Stack the warm tortillas on a cutting board. One at a time, fill each tortilla with the chicken. Roll up and place seam-side down in the saucy pan. Repeat until the pan is nice and full.

4. Cover everything with the rest of the enchilada sauce. Top with cheese, if you like.

5. Bake for 30 to 40 minutes until cooked through. The tortillas will be slightly crispy, and the cheese will be melted, if using.

6. Garnish with tomatoes, olives, and jalapeños.

Note: *An easy way to shred chicken is to use a stand or hand mixer. Place the chicken in a large mixing bowl. Cover the mixer and bowl with a kitchen towel. Beat it at low speed until the meat is pulled apart.*

a healthier home cook

Refried Beans

Yield: Serves 4

Ingredients:

1 pound (454 g) dried pinto beans, soaked overnight (see note)

Bone Broth (page 149) or filtered water

1 medium onion, diced

1 teaspoon sea salt

1 teaspoon ground cumin

1 teaspoon garlic powder

Note: *To soak the beans, add to a glass container with filtered water and a splash of apple cider vinegar. Let sit overnight.*

1. In an Instant Pot, add the soaked beans and enough liquid to come up ½ inch (1.3 cm) above. Add the onions, salt, cumin, and garlic powder.

2. Close and seal the Instant Pot and set it for 13 minutes.

3. Release the pressure, then drain the beans, reserving some of the liquid.

4. Mash the beans by hand or use an immersion blender until you get the consistency you want. Add some of the reserved liquid if you need to thin the mixture. Taste and adjust the seasoning if needed.

Taqueria-Style Roasted Carrots

Yield: Serves 4

Ingredients:

1 tablespoon (15 ml) avocado oil or olive oil

¼ teaspoon ground cumin

¼ teaspoon dried oregano

½–1 teaspoon sea salt

⅛ teaspoon black pepper

4–5 medium carrots, sliced

1 small onion or 2 medium shallots, sliced

2 cloves garlic, thinly sliced, minced, or pressed

⅔ cup (85 g) jarred pickled jalapeños (see note)

½ cup (8 g) fresh cilantro leaves, plus more for serving (optional)

1. Preheat the oven to 350°F (175°C). Line a baking sheet with parchment paper.

2. In a large bowl, whisk together the oil and seasonings.

3. Add the remaining ingredients, and toss to coat well. Spread everything out on the baking sheet.

4. Roast for 30 to 40 minutes until the carrots are as tender as you like them.

Note: *If you want a portion without jalapeños for little ones or the spicy resistant: Leave the jalapeños out. Mix together all other ingredients, then scoop out a portion onto one side of your baking sheet. Add the jalapeños to the remaining portion, mix, and put it on the other side of the pan.*

Chimichurri Beef Pasta

Sometimes the most random meals come together and end up becoming a repeat dish. This is one of them in my house. I basically invented this recipe because I had too many leftover herbs. It's a simple recipe, made bright and flavorful by those herbs. After playing with the base recipe a few times, I found I could make it more nutrient dense and increase pepperiness by adding the arugula.

Yield: Serves 4

Ingredients for the Chimichurri:

2 very generous handfuls of arugula
2 generous handfuls of fresh
   flat-leaf parsley
1 big handful of fresh cilantro
Zest and juice of 1 lemon
Sprinkle of crushed red pepper
2 medium shallots
1–2 cloves garlic
Sea salt and black pepper, to taste
1 teaspoon dried oregano
2 tablespoons (30 ml) red wine
   vinegar
¼–⅓ cup (59–79 ml) extra-virgin
   olive oil, depending on your desired
   consistency

Ingredients for the Beef Pasta:

1 box (12 ounces, or 340 g)
   gluten-free pasta, such as farfalle
   or penne
1 pound (454 g) pasture-raised
   ground beef
½ teaspoon ground turmeric
Sea salt and black pepper, to taste
½ teaspoon garlic powder
½ teaspoon onion powder
⅛ teaspoon ground coriander
⅛ teaspoon ground mustard

Optional:

Vegetables (Sliced bell pepper and
   quartered cherry tomatoes are good
   additions.)

For Serving:

Hot sauce

Make the Chimichurri:

1. In a food processor, add all the chimichurri ingredients except the olive oil. Blend until combined.

2. While the motor is running, drizzle in the olive oil until you have a thick sauce.

Make the Beef Pasta:

1. In a pot of boiling salted water, cook the pasta according to the package directions. Drain and set aside.

2. Meanwhile, in a 10-inch (25-cm) skillet, sauté the ground beef until browned. Make a well in the center, add the turmeric to toast, then sauté for 1 to 2 minutes.

3. Season with the salt and pepper, garlic and onion powders, coriander, and mustard. Sauté for about 30 seconds to combine.

4. Add the veggies if using, and cook until slightly tender.

5. In a serving dish, combine the meat mixture with the cooked noodles. Add the chimichurri, and mix gently to coat.

6. Serve with hot sauce of your choice.

Mississippi Pot Roast

I think the algorithm was telling me to make Mississippi Pot Roast at one point because it kept getting recommended to me. Once I looked into it, I saw its key ingredients for flavor are a packet of gravy mix, a packet of ranch mix, and a jar of pepperoncini. Well once I saw the ranch seasoning packet, I knew it was meant to be because I love making my own powdered ranch! And after making the whole dish, I totally got the hype.

Yield: Serves 4

Ingredients:

1 tablespoon (15 ml) extra-virgin olive oil

1 (4–6 pound [2.3–2.7 kg]) pasture-raised chuck roast

1 medium onion, diced

1 jar (15½ ounces, or 439 g) pepperoncini with liquid, or to taste depending on your preferred spice level

6 tablespoons (89 ml) Ranch Packet Seasoning Blend (recipe follows)

1 cup (237 ml) Bone Broth (page 149)

3–4 tablespoons (43–57 g) salted butter or ghee

2–3 tablespoons (15–23 g) tapioca flour or arrowroot

For Serving:

Mashed potatoes, baked potato, cauliflower rice, rice, mashed cauliflower, or mashed sweet potatoes

Make in a Dutch Oven:

1. Preheat the oven to 400°F (200°C).

2. In a Dutch oven, heat the olive oil over medium heat and sear the meat on all sides. Add the onions, pepperoncini and liquid, ranch seasonings, broth, and butter.

3. Cover and cook it in the oven for 1 hour. Then lower the heat to 300°F (150°C), and cook for 3 hours.

4. Take it out of the oven, and remove the meat to a cutting board. When cool enough to handle, shred the meat and place it on a serving dish.

5. Whisk in the tapioca flour a little at a time until you reach the consistency you like for the gravy. It will continue to thicken a bit as it cools, so don't go too wild.

6. Spoon the gravy over the meat, and serve.

Make in an Instant Pot:

1. Set the Instant Pot to sauté, add the olive oil, and let heat for about 30 seconds. Add the meat, and sear it for 3 to 4 minutes on each side.

2. Add everything else to the Instant Pot and pressure-cook on high for 1 hour. Use the manual or auto release.

continued on following page

3. Remove the meat to a cutting board. When cool enough to handle, shred the meat and place it on a serving dish.

4. Press the sauté button on your electric pressure cooker. Once the mixture is bubbling, be careful not to let it burn. Whisk in the tapioca flour a little at a time until you reach the consistency you like for the gravy. It will continue to thicken a bit as it cools, so don't go too wild.

5. Serve with the potatoes or rice of choice. Drizzle with the gravy, and top with more pepperoncini if you like.

Ranch Packet Seasoning Blend

Mix up all the dried-herb goodness, then store it or use it as you see fit. These measurements make a one-packet equivalent. I often double or triple it, throwing one serving right into 16 ounces (454 g) of sour cream for a dip.

Yield: Makes about ⅓ cup

Ingredients:
3 tablespoons (44 ml) dried parsley
2 teaspoons (2 g) dried chives
2 teaspoons (2 g) dried dill
1 teaspoon garlic powder
2½ teaspoons (5 g) onion powder
1 teaspoon sea salt
½ teaspoon black pepper
½ teaspoon coconut sugar

1. To a repurposed mason jar or spice jar with lid, add all the ingredients.

2. Put on the lid, then give it a good shake to combine it thoroughly.

Tip: *The ranch seasoning recipe is easily doubled or tripled to use for all things.*

Cottage Pie

This is a weeknight meal around here, because you can absolutely prep it the night before or in the morning and heat it up come dinnertime. You can even cook it to order in two smaller dishes. It's a hearty dish and a crowd-pleaser as well.

Some recipes I've seen don't add egg to the potatoes, but I think it makes it way better, keeping the potatoes more in their own little shelf on top. I also think the stew part only gets better the next day, marrying like a stew. The tapioca flour will thicken up the sauce and make it a gravy, and help it hold together after cooking, not being too runny.

Yield: Serves 4

Ingredients:

1 pound (454 g) pasture-raised ground meat (I usually use beef. Turkey, chicken, or lamb also work well for a shepherd's pie.)

1 medium onion, diced

3–5 cloves garlic, pressed

5 large carrots, diced

4 stalks celery, diced

1 teaspoon avocado oil

¼–½ teaspoon ground turmeric

3 cups (495 g) frozen vegetables (I like peas and green beans.)

¼ teaspoon ground mustard

¼ teaspoon garlic powder

¼ teaspoon onion powder

¼ teaspoon dried oregano

¼ teaspoon dried coriander

½ teaspoon paprika, plus more for sprinkling on top

Dash of cayenne pepper

Sea salt and black pepper, to taste

1 teaspoon Worcestershire sauce

1 cup (59 ml) Bone Broth (page 149)

1 tablespoon (15 ml) tapioca flour, or more if needed

Mashed potatoes (see note)

1. Preheat the oven to 350°F (175°C).

2. In a large skillet, brown the ground meat over medium heat. Add in the onions, and sauté for about 5 minutes until translucent.

3. Add the garlic, carrots, and celery. Once those are getting a bit tender, make a well in the middle of your pan. Add the oil, sprinkle in the turmeric, and toast it for a minute or two.

4. Add in the vegetables, then toss gently to combine.

5. Add the mustard, garlic and onion powders, oregano, coriander, paprika, and a little dash of cayenne. Season everything well with salt and pepper. Drizzle in the Worcestershire, and stir to combine.

6. In a measuring cup, add the broth, and whisk in the tapioca flour. Add this to the skillet.

7. Let it simmer for a few minutes to thicken. You want an ooey gooey texture here; if it's not thick enough, whisk in more tapioca and heat it to thicken.

continued on following page

8. Add the meat and vegetable mixture to a 9 × 13-inch (23 × 33-cm) pan (or similar size). Spread the mashed potatoes over the top. Sprinkle with a little paprika.

9. Bake for 40 minutes. Remove from the oven, and let rest for 10 minutes before serving.

Note: *To make the mashed potatoes quickly and easily, make them in an Instant Pot. You will need 8 to 10 Yukon gold potatoes (about 5 to 6 cups diced [550 to 660 g]), 1 cup (59 ml) of water or broth, 4 tablespoons (57 g) of butter, salt,*

black pepper, garlic powder, and 1 large egg. The egg helps the potatoes stiffen and hold together on top of the dish.

Rinse the potatoes and add them whole to your Instant Pot. Add the liquid, seal, and pressure-cook for 6 minutes. Leave on the "keep warm" setting until ready to mash and use. When ready to top the shepherd's pie, add the butter and the salt, pepper, and garlic powder to taste. Mash well. Crack the egg in a separate bowl, and add some warm mashed potatoes; this gently heats or "tempers" the egg. Gently mix. Add the tempered egg to your mashed potatoes, and mix well.

Pasta Pot

My husband, Damien, is the architect behind this recipe. So, yes, it's mostly pantry staples and stuff he found in the fridge . . . and is sort of inspired by a certain packaged hamburger-assistant-type product. But together with the Hearty Sprouted Grains Bowl on page 65, I just had to include it in the book. They are both go-to recipes that save you from processed convenience foods or takeout on those nights when you don't want to spend the money. If you make it as written, it's totally great—but it's very flexible! Omit the meat and it eats like a warm pasta salad. Or mix up the mix-ins: Try bell pepper, roasted red pepper, artichoke heart, or capers!

Important note: If you have kids, I recommend pairing this recipe with the children's book *Strega Nona*, by Tomie dePaola . . . it inspired the name!

Yield: Serves 4

Ingredients:

1 teaspoon extra-virgin olive oil
1 medium yellow onion, diced
Optional: 1 pound (454 g) grass-fed or pasture-raised ground meat
3–5 cloves garlic, pressed
¼ teaspoon ground turmeric
⅛ teaspoon ground coriander
⅛ teaspoon ground mustard
¼ teaspoon paprika
¼ teaspoon onion powder
¼ teaspoon garlic powder
½ teaspoon dried oregano
Sea salt and black pepper, to taste
8 ounces (227 g) frozen spinach
1–2 cups (200–400 g) chopped tomatoes
½–1 cup (360–720 g) sliced kalamata olives
1 box (12 ounces, or 340 g) gluten-free pasta, cooked and drained

1. In a medium stockpot, heat the olive oil over medium-low heat. Add the onions, and sauté until tender.

2. Add the ground meat (if using), and cook until browned.

3. Add the garlic, and cook for 1 to 2 minutes.

4. Make a well in the center of the pan, add the turmeric, and toast it for 2 to 3 minutes.

5. Add the seasonings, and sauté until combined, about 1 minute.

6. Add the spinach, tomatoes, and kalamata olives. Cook for 5 to 10 minutes until everything is hot and tender.

7. Toss with the cooked pasta, and serve.

House Bolognese

This is my take on a classic plate of spaghetti, but of course I added a bunch of frozen spinach to mine for vitamins and minerals. I do a couple other unique things as well, adding toasted turmeric in there, a pinch of cinnamon, coriander, and mustard. It might sound weird, but it works . . . it's sort of my everyday blend meets Italian. Don't worry—it's all subtle and over the years has become one of the more popular recipes I've shared.

Yield: Serves 4

Ingredients:

1 box (12 ounces, or 340 g) gluten-free noodles of choice

1 tablespoon (15 ml) extra-virgin olive oil or avocado oil, plus more if needed

1 medium yellow onion, diced

3–5 cloves garlic, pressed

1 pound (454 g) pasture-raised ground meat of choice, or 2 cups (150 g) cooked lentils for a meat-free version

½–1 teaspoon ground turmeric

2 tablespoons (30 ml) tomato paste

1 bag (12 to 16 ounces, or 340 to 454 g) frozen spinach

1 jar (16 ounces, or 454 g) diced tomatoes

¼ teaspoon ground mustard

⅛ teaspoon ground coriander

Pinch of crushed red pepper or cayenne pepper

¼ teaspoon dried or ½ teaspoon fresh rosemary

½ teaspoon dried oregano

⅛ teaspoon ground cinnamon

½ teaspoon dried basil

½ teaspoon dried thyme

Sea salt and black pepper, to taste

For Serving:
Freshly grated Parmesan cheese

1. In a pot of boiling salted water, cook the pasta until al dente. Drain and set aside.

2. In a heavy-bottomed pan, warm the oil over medium-low heat. Add the onions, and sauté for 3 to 5 minutes until translucent. Add the garlic, and sauté for 1 minute.

3. Add the meat, if using, and cook through.

4. Move everything to the sides to create a well. Add more oil, if needed, then add the turmeric, and toast it for a couple of minutes.

5. Make a new well, and toast the tomato paste the same way.

6. Add the rest of the ingredients. (If you're using lentils, add those, too.) Bring up to a boil, lower to a simmer, and let simmer for at least 1 hour, stirring occasionally.

7. Add the cooked noodles to the finished sauce. Top with the Parmesan, and enjoy!

Bacon-Wrapped Meatloaf with Crispy Smashed Potatoes and Grilled Artichoke

Growing up, meatloaf never sounded appetizing and I feel like it was even made fun of as a less-than-appetizing dinner. So, I don't know what possessed me to make it as an adult. I have to say though, the whole family is glad I did! The bacon is a must, and the sauce is a sweet and savory addition that brings it all together. It's easiest to mix with your hands. If that grosses you out, that's okay. You can use a big spoon. (I find it sort of soothing.)

Yield: Serves 4

Ingredients for the Meatloaf:

2 large eggs

½ cup (113 g) plain yogurt

2 teaspoons (10 g) Dijon mustard

2 teaspoons (10 ml) Worcestershire sauce

1 teaspoon sea salt

½ teaspoon black pepper

½ teaspoon dried thyme

½ teaspoon paprika

2 tablespoons (30 ml) extra-virgin olive oil

1 medium yellow onion, diced

2–3 cloves garlic, pressed

2 pounds (908 g) pasture-raised ground meat (I like either: 1 pound beef, ½ pound lamb, ½ pound pork; 2:1 beef and pork; or all beef. It's completely up to you!)

⅓ cup (37 g) almond flour, as needed

Make the Meatloaf:

1. Preheat the oven to 350°F (175°C). Line a baking sheet with parchment paper.

2. In a large bowl, whisk the eggs, yogurt, mustard, Worcestershire, and seasonings.

3. In a small skillet, heat the olive oil over medium heat. Add the onions. Sauté for 3 to 5 minutes until translucent, adding the garlic during the last minute of cooking.

4. Add the cooked onions and garlic to the bowl. Add the meat, then mix everything well.

5. Add the almond flour a little at a time until the mix holds together and does not stick to the sides of the bowl. You may not need all the almond flour.

6. Form the mixture into a loaf about 5 × 12 inches (13 × 30 cm) on the lined sheet.

continued on following page

Ingredients for the Glaze:

⅓ cup (90 g) ketchup

2 tablespoons (30 ml) coconut sugar

2 teaspoons (10 ml) apple
cider vinegar

10–16 ounces (284–454 g) bacon

For Serving:

Crispy Smashed Potatoes
(recipe follows)

Grilled Artichokes with Garlic
Lemon Aioli (page 169)

7. Cover the meatloaf with the glaze. Place strips of bacon crosswise on top so they overlap, tucking the ends under the loaf. It's okay if they don't overlap.

8. Bake for about 1 hour until the internal temperature is 160°F (70°C). Let it rest for 15 minutes before cutting and serving.

Note: For people that like sauce, here's an idea: Double the glaze recipe, reserving half for serving alongside the meatloaf.

Crispy Smashed Potatoes

This was one of the first recipes my daughter Abigail made with minimal help from mom. (Basically I handled the hot stuff!)

Yield: Serves 4+

Ingredients:

1½ pounds (680 g) potatoes (gold, red, or other small varieties), cooked fork-tender (see note), kept hot

1 tablespoon (15 ml) fat, such as salted butter, extra-virgin olive oil, or bacon fat

Sea salt and black pepper, to taste

Seasoning such as garlic powder or seasoning salt, to taste

1. Preheat the oven to 400°F (200°C). Line a baking sheet with parchment paper.

2. In a large bowl, toss the hot potatoes with the fat and seasonings.

3. Place on the baking sheet. Using the bottom of a mug or cup, press the potatoes until about ½ inch (1.3 cm) thick.

4. Bake for 25 to 30 minutes. Crank the oven to broil for the last few minutes until the potatoes are nice and crispy and golden brown. Keep a close eye to avoid burning.

Note: Utilizing the Instant Pot to hack this recipe is a game changer. Pressure-cook your gold, red, or similar small potatoes for 3 to 4 minutes on the rack or in the steamer basket. If you don't have an Instant Pot, you can boil your taters in water on the stovetop for about 20 minutes until fork-tender, then drain.

Grilled Artichokes with Garlic Lemon Aioli

Artichokes are delicious and fun to eat, and they're also a powerhouse of nutrition. They are high in antioxidants, a good source of iron, rich in minerals and vitamins (A, B₆, C, E, K . . .), promote liver detoxification, have a high-fiber content, support heart health and immunity, and promote healthy skin.

Yield: Serves 4

Ingredients:
2 whole artichokes
1 teaspoon sea salt
1 lemon
1 teaspoon extra-virgin olive oil
Garlic pepper, to taste

For Serving:
Garlic Lemon Aioli (recipe follows)

Note: *You can also use a grill-style pan if you don't have a grill.*

1. Give the artichokes a good rinse. Trim off the top and any sharp points using kitchen shears.

2. Fill a wide pot with a couple inches (5 cm) of water. Set it over high heat to boil. Add the artichokes, salt, and the juice and rind of the lemon.

3. Lower the heat to a simmer. Cover and let steam for 30 minutes. Remove to a colander to drain, and let rest until cool to touch.

4. Preheat a grill to medium heat. Cut the artichokes in half lengthwise and remove the fuzzy "choke" with a spoon; a grape-fruit spoon or melon baller work well. Drizzle with the oil and season with some garlic pepper.

5. Grill each side over medium-high heat for 2 to 4 minutes to get a light char.

6. Serve with the aioli.

Garlic Lemon Aioli

Yield: Serves 4

Ingredients:
1 cup (208 g) mayonnaise (store-bought or homemade, page 69)
Zest of 1 lemon
Juice of half of a lemon
¼ teaspoon sea salt
¼ teaspoon garlic pepper
2 cloves garlic, pressed

1. In a small bowl, combine all the ingredients.

2. Let that marry for 30 minutes or more in the refrigerator before serving.

Grain-Free Meatballs with Roasted Cauliflower

These are a great dinner, and you can easily make a big batch and freeze these meatballs, making them great for parties and such. And they are a crowd-pleaser. Use any ground meat you like for this. Pasture-raised ground beef, turkey, chicken, or lamb all work on their own or as blends. You can serve them with pasta or a variety of sauces, or add them to a soup—you name it. We also like these with in-season vegetables and Whole Roasted Cauliflower (page 171).

Yield: Makes about 2 dozen meatballs

Ingredients:

1 large egg

½ teaspoon mustard (any kind)

½ teaspoon ketchup

½ teaspoon dried oregano

½ teaspoon dried thyme

½ teaspoon onion powder

½ teaspoon garlic powder

1 teaspoon extra-virgin olive oil

About ¼ cup (28 g) almond flour or coconut flour

1 pound (454 g) ground meat of choice

1. Preheat the oven to 350°F (175°C). Line a baking sheet with parchment paper. In a large bowl, whisk together all the ingredients except the ground meat.

2. Add the meat. Stir to combine with a spoon or your hands until the mixture sticks together and pulls away from the sides of the bowl. Add a little bit of oil if too dry or more flour if too wet.

3. Use a small scoop or teaspoon to make meatballs of the same size. Form them into balls and place them on the lined sheet.

4. Bake for about 18 minutes until the internal temperature reaches 160°F (70°C). Serve as desired.

Whole Roasted Cauliflower

Simple. Beautiful. Delicious. When you have a whole cauliflower in need of a recipe, give this a try.

Yield: Serves 4

Ingredients:

1 whole head cauliflower

2–3 tablespoons (30–44 ml) fat, such as butter, extra-virgin olive oil, or bacon fat

1 teaspoon sea salt

Optional: 1 teaspoon garlic powder, or other seasoning of choice

1. Preheat the oven to 350°F (175°C). Trim the stalk of the cauliflower so the head can sit flat.

2. Place the cauliflower stem-side down in a cast-iron skillet or other oven-safe pan. Smear with the fat, coating it well. Sprinkle with the salt and any other seasoning, if using.

3. Pop in the oven for about 1 hour until tender and golden brown.

4. Slice into steaks or cut into florets, and enjoy.

Chapter 7

Sweets and Sips

Grain-Free Carrot Cake
with Cream Cheese Frosting

I don't make a ton of cakes from scratch, and I'm also not against good-quality box mixes—so what's the story here? Sure, it's grain-free and refined-sugar-free, and it is 100 percent delicious. But why is the only cake in this book a carrot cake? Well, I have made a carrot cake every year for too many years to count for my mother-in-law's birthday. It all started because she loves carrot cake and I eat gluten-free, so I had to figure out a way to make it happen. Now even my friends that scoff at gluten-free anything have been converted to this as the ultimate carrot cake.

Yield: Makes one 2-layer, 9-inch (23-cm) cake

Ingredients for the Cake:

7 large eggs

1¾ cups (213 g) coconut sugar

1½ teaspoons vanilla extract

4½ cups (432 g) almond flour

2 teaspoons (9 g) salt

1½ teaspoons baking powder

¾ teaspoon baking soda

1½ teaspoons ground cardamom

1½ teaspoons ground cinnamon

1½ teaspoons ground ginger

About 5 medium-large carrots, finely shredded

¾ cup (59 ml) avocado or coconut oil

Optional:

1 cup (100 g) shredded coconut

1 cup (125 g) chopped pecans, plus more for topping cake if desired

Make the Cake:

1. Preheat the oven to 350°F (175°C). Grease two 9-inch (23-cm) cake pans, and place a circle of parchment paper in the bottom of each.

2. With a mixer on medium speed, beat the eggs and coconut sugar for about 5 minutes until the mixture is very creamy, smooth, and light.

3. Add the vanilla, and mix briefly to incorporate.

4. In a separate bowl, combine the almond flour, salt, baking powder, baking soda, and spices.

5. In a third bowl, combine the carrots, and, if using, the coconut and pecans.

6. To the egg mix, add some dry mix, then some carrot mix, then some more dry mix; stir between each addition until it's all well combined.

7. Pour this batter into the cake pans. Bake for 35 to 45 minutes until a toothpick comes out clean.

continued on following page

Ingredients for the Frosting:

12 ounces (340 g) cream cheese,
  room temperature

½ cup (1 stick, or 113 g)
  salted butter, room temperature

1 teaspoon vanilla extract

¼ cup (59 ml) maple syrup,
  or to taste

Pinch of sea salt

Optional:

¼–1 cup (30–120 g) tapioca
  flour to thicken if you prefer
  a firmer frosting

8. Let the cakes cool on a baking rack for
   10 minutes before removing from the
   pans. Then let them cool completely on
   a wire rack before frosting.

Make the Frosting:

1. In the mixer, beat together all the ingredients until well combined and smooth.

Frost the Cake:

1. Using an inverted spatula or knife, spread
   the top of one cake with a thick layer of
   frosting. Layer the other cake on top, with
   the top side down, to give a flat surface to
   the top of the whole cake.

2. Cover the entire cake with as much or
   little of the frosting as you like. Start with
   a crumb coat all over, then add more
   frosting to the top or sides. I like to leave a
   more exposed edge around the sides.

3. Add more pecans all around the edge of
   the top layer, if using.

Tip: *You can refrigerate the frosting for up
to 1 week. Let it come to room temperature
before frosting your cake.*

Paleo Chocolate Chip Cookies

These are one of the first things I learned to make when I went on my health journey. They are so, so good, and certainly passable to the non-gluten-free crowd. I remember them being a hit at my book club! Because gluten-free chocolate chip cookies are notoriously hard to make, I feel like I got lucky. I was sent a recipe from a friend and after making a few modifications it pretty much worked perfectly the first time. It's deliciously chewy and moist.

Yield: Makes about 2 dozen

Ingredients:

2⅔ cups (160 g) blanched
  almond flour
1 teaspoon baking soda
½ teaspoon ground cinnamon
½ teaspoon sea salt
2 large eggs
2 teaspoons (10 ml) vanilla extract
½ cup (118 ml) maple syrup
½ cup (118 ml) melted coconut oil
½ cup (90 g) semisweet
  chocolate chips

1. Preheat the oven to 350°F (175°C). Line two cookie sheets with parchment paper.

2. In a large bowl, whisk together the dry ingredients.

3. In a separate bowl, combine the eggs, vanilla, and maple syrup.

4. Pour the wet ingredients into the dry ingredients, and combine using a wooden spoon.

5. Add the melted coconut oil and chocolate chips, and stir to combine.

6. Scoop the dough onto the lined cookie sheets, spacing the cookies about 1 inch (2.5 cm) apart. I use a small—about 2-inch (5-cm)—ice cream scoop, but you can use teaspoons. Tap the bottom of the cookie sheet on the counter to help the dough flatten a smidge.

7. Bake for 13 minutes until slightly golden around the edges. Place the pans on baking racks, and let them cool for about 5 minutes until releasing.

Candy Bar Dates

This started as a viral recipe that got me hooked. My son Ezekiel is a date fanatic, and I had to give it a go. It's very easy to make, and you'd be surprised just how much the chewiness of the dates gives each bite a nougat-like texture. Make a big batch and keep them in the fridge. You can also freeze them if you are the type of person to enjoy that; I don't do it with mine but only because they hurt my teeth!

Yield: Makes 1 dozen

Ingredients:

12 dates

¼ cup (60 g) nut or seed butter

¼ cup (38 g) chopped nuts or sprouted seeds

½ cup (90 g) semisweet chocolate chips

1 teaspoon coconut oil

Flaky salt, for sprinkling

1. Line a baking sheet with parchment paper. Open a date and remove the pit if it has one. Repeat with all of the dates.

2. Fill each date with the nut butter, about ½ teaspoon per date.

3. Add a sprinkle of nuts on top of the nut butter.

4. In the top of a double boiler, melt the chocolate chips and coconut oil. Stir the chocolate until it's completely melted, then turn off the heat.

5. Take the dates and dunk them into the chocolate until they are lightly coated. Place them on the lined baking sheet.

6. Sprinkle with the flaky salt.

7. Pop them in the fridge to set. You can use the freezer if you're in a hurry or like them frozen.

How to Store: *Store in an airtight container in the refrigerator for up to 1 week.*

Tip: *A double boiler is one of the best ways to melt chocolate. Fill a small saucepan with 1 to 2 inches (2.5 to 5 cm) of water. Use a glass or stainless steel mixing bowl that fits snugly on top of your saucepan without touching the water underneath. Bring the water to a simmer, and add the chocolate and coconut oil to the bowl on top.*

Dairy-Free Caramel Corn

You know those tubs that go around at Christmas with three sections of popcorn? My favorite section was always caramel corn. It's no surprise that eventually I had to hunt down and research how to make it, then put my ALLT spin on it. I love that you can taste the maple in this as well; it really sets it apart from store-bought.

Yield: Serves 4

Ingredients:

3 tablespoons (45 ml) coconut oil, divided

⅓ cup (73 g) popcorn kernels

½ cup (118 ml) maple syrup

¼ teaspoon sea salt

1 teaspoon vanilla extract

1. Heat a heavy-bottom pan with a lid over medium heat for 3 to 5 minutes. Melt 2 tablespoons (30 ml) of the coconut oil, add just three popcorn kernels, and cover.

2. Give the pan a gentle shake periodically. When all three kernels have popped, add the remaining kernels and cover. Shake the pan gently and remove it from the heat for 30 seconds.

3. Return it to the heat, and cook the popcorn until the popping slows to almost nothing. Remove the pan from the heat. Leave it covered for 30 seconds.

4. Meanwhile, in a small saucepan over medium-low heat, add the remaining 1 tablespoon (15 ml) of coconut oil, the maple syrup, and the salt. Bring to a simmer and cook for a couple minutes to thicken, making sure not to let it burn.

5. Turn off the heat, and stir in the vanilla.

6. Pour that goodness over your freshly popped corn. Stir to coat.

a healthier home cook

Frost It, Top It, Dip It:
My Coconut Whipped Cream, Pressure-Cooked Caramel, and Dye-Free Berry Buttercream

Whether it's a kid's birthday and I need something for box-mix cupcakes or it's a cold day and I am making hot cocoa, from the earliest moment in my ALLT journey I found there were a few things that, while not a full recipe on their own, I was reaching for again and again in my kitchen.

Coconut Whipped Cream

I always keep a can of organic coconut cream in my refrigerator. You just never know when you're going to need some whipped cream. And it makes an amazing, healthy-fat, delicious addition to so many things when you want a sweet treat.

Just have fun! You can swap out coconut sugar for no sweetener or monk fruit or maple syrup or honey if that's what you have. It's seriously simple, very nourishing, easily transformable, and delicious.

I make many variations of this, depending on what I'm serving it with or am in the mood for. Here are a few recipes:

Yield: Serves 4

Ingredients for the Base:

1 can (13½ ounces, or 383 g) coconut cream, refrigerated at least overnight and drained of any liquid

½ teaspoon vanilla bean powder or vanilla extract

Pinch of sea salt

Ingredients for Variation #1:

1 teaspoon ground cinnamon

1 teaspoon maple syrup

Ingredient for Variation #2:

1 teaspoon coconut sugar

Ingredients for Variation #3:

1 teaspoon coconut sugar

1 teaspoon cacao powder

Ingredient for Variation #4:

1 teaspoon ground freeze-dried berries

1. In a large mixing bowl or the bowl of a stand mixer, combine the chilled and drained coconut cream with the vanilla bean extract or powder and salt.

2. Add the additional ingredients from the variation of choice.

3. Using a hand mixer or stand mixer, beat for 2 to 4 minutes until thick.

4. Use immediately, or store it in the fridge until ready to use.

continued on following page

Pressure-Cooked Caramel

There was a time when I went more than seven years not eating legit caramel because it made me sick. I have such a precise amount of time measured because caramel is one of my ultimate favorite things. Now my only question is why on earth did I not figure this out sooner?! With the help of an electric pressure cooker, I can now eat caramel made from just three simple ingredients.

Drizzle this over vanilla ice cream, bananas, coffee, an ice-blended matcha . . . the possibilities are endless.

Yield: Serves 4

Ingredients:

1 can (14 ounces, or 396 g) sweetened condensed milk
1 teaspoon vanilla extract
Pinch of sea salt

Note: *You can also use sweetened condensed coconut milk for a dairy-free option, but note the adjustment to the cook time in the instructions. The dairy version is thicker, but the coconut version makes for a delicious drizzle.*

Instant Pot Method:

1. Pour the contents of the can into a mason jar. I used a pint-size, wide-mouth mason jar. Cover it tightly with foil, or screw on the metal seal and ring lid.

2. Add the wire rack to an Instant Pot. Place the closed jar in the center of the rack. Pour water into the Instant Pot until it covers at least half of the jar.

3. Close, seal, and set to pressure-cook for 16 minutes. For sweetened condensed coconut milk, set to pressure-cook for 45 minutes.

4. Release the pressure, open the lid of the pressure cooker once it's safe to do so. You don't want to leave the jar in that scalding water long. Carefully remove jar with tongs or oven mitts to a safe surface to cool.

5. Let the jar cool until it's comfortable to hold—the caramel will be quite hot at first! Once you're able to remove the lid, pour out the contents into a small bowl. Stir in the vanilla and salt.

Note: *Using a hand mixer to mix for one minute gives it a wonderful texture.*

6. Use immediately, or store it in the refrigerator to thicken.

Oven Method:

1. Preheat the oven to 425° (220°C). Remove the label and lid from the can, place the can in an oven-safe dish, and cover tightly with foil. Place the dish in a larger pan and fill it with 1 inch (2.5 cm) or so of water.

2. Bake for about 1 hour and 30 minutes. Let sit until cool enough to handle, then pour out the contents into a bowl. Stir in the vanilla and salt.

Stovetop Method:

1. Remove the label from the can, but leave the lid intact. Lay down the can in a pot, then cover it completely by 2 inches (5 cm) of water.

2. Place the pot over high heat and bring it to boil. Lower the heat and simmer for 3 to 4 hours.

3. Let it sit until cool enough to handle, then pour out the contents into a small bowl. Stir in the vanilla and salt.

Tip: *You can also use a slow cooker: Follow the stovetop steps, and set the cooker to low heat for 8 to 10 hours.*

Dye-Free Berry Buttercream

This is a very traditional buttercream. It can be easily adjusted to be various flavors and colors. I've made pinks and purples with ground up freeze-dried berries, blue with powdered blue spirulina, and orange with freeze-dried carrots.

Yield: Makes 1 dozen cupcakes

Ingredients:

2 cups (4 sticks, or 450 g) salted butter, room temperature

1 teaspoon vanilla extract

4½ cups (518 g) powdered sugar, sifted (see note)

2 tablespoons (30 ml) cream or nut milk for dairy-free

Pinch of sea salt

Note: *Sift your powdered sugar to remove any clumps and create a smoother consistency. You can sift it into a separate bowl or right into your butter mixture.*

1. In a large bowl using a hand mixer, or in the bowl of a stand mixer, beat the butter for about 2 minutes until smooth.

2. Add the vanilla. Beat for 1 minute until fully incorporated.

3. Add the sifted powdered sugar. Beat on low speed until combined.

4. Add the cream, then beat for 3 to 4 minutes until fully combined. Add a pinch of salt, then beat again for 1 minute.

How to Store: *Place the buttercream in an airtight container, and keep it in the refrigerator for up to 1 week. Let it come to room temperature before frosting your cake. To make a fluffier consistency, I like to beat the frosting one more time before adding it to a piping bag or icing my cake.*

Chocolate Pudding with Raw Honey Whipped Cream

Now yes, there are other pudding recipes out there that meet the ALLT guidelines and deliver more of a classic, custardy chocolate pudding. But they are involved. This on the other hand is simply a delicious replacement for the instant pudding pack. It's an "I need pudding tonight" fixer. The secret is the arrowroot or tapioca flour.

Yield: Serves 4

Ingredients:

4 cups (960 ml) milk or 2½ cans (13½ ounces, or 400 ml) unsweetened canned coconut milk

½ cup (30 g) arrowroot or tapioca flour

3 tablespoons (19 g) raw cacao powder

⅓ cup (75 g) coconut sugar

About ⅔ cup (115 g) semisweet chocolate chips

1 teaspoon vanilla extract

For Serving:

Raw Honey Whipped Cream (recipe follows)

1. In a medium saucepan, heat the milk over medium-low heat.

2. Meanwhile, in a medium bowl, whisk together the arrowroot, cacao powder, and coconut sugar.

3. Add these dry ingredients to the pan with the milk, and cook for about 10 minutes, whisking occasionally, until you achieve a thick, smooth, and creamy consistency.

4. Add the chocolate chips, and stir until they are melted. Turn off the heat. Stir in the vanilla.

5. Serve warm, or chill it in the refrigerator and serve when it is cold.

Raw Honey Whipped Cream

Yield: Makes 2 cups

Ingredients:

1 cup (237 ml) heavy cream, very cold

¼ teaspoon vanilla extract

1 tablespoon (15 ml) raw honey

Small pinch of sea salt

1. In a large bowl, whisk together all the ingredients by hand. Alternatively, use a handheld mixer on medium-high speed for 2 to 3 minutes until the whipped cream is thick and fluffy.

2. Serve immediately or as close to serving time as possible.

Tip: *If you have the extra time, chill a bowl and beaters in the freezer for 10 minutes beforehand. It makes it easier to whip, and it helps the whipped cream hold its shape.*

Maple-Cinnamon Marshmallows

Marshmallows should be simple sweets. The problem is most big brands have ingredients I don't like: carrageenan, corn syrup, preservatives, natural and artificial flavors, and sometimes a dash of blue food coloring (to enhance the white). Recipe research to the rescue! Now we can eat marshmallows as a more wholesome treat.

Yield: Serves 4

Ingredients:

1 cup (236 ml) water, divided

3 tablespoons (44 ml) grass-fed gelatin

1 cup (237 ml) maple syrup

¼ teaspoon Himalayan salt

Powdered sugar or arrowroot, for dusting pan

1 teaspoon vanilla extract

1 teaspoon ground cinnamon

Note: *Using arrowroot instead of powdered sugar will make this recipe free of refined sugar.*

How to Store: *Store these at room temperature in an airtight container for 1 to 2 days, or in the freezer for up to 3 months. They won't freeze solid due to the gelatin, and they're pretty fun straight out of the freezer.*

1. In a large bowl, add ½ cup (118 ml) of water and sprinkle the grass-fed gelatin on top. Don't stir. Just leave it to "bloom."

2. In a medium saucepan, bring the maple syrup, remaining water, and Himalayan salt to a boil.

3. Keep an eye on it, and let it simmer to reach the "soft ball" stage (about 240°F [115°C]). A candy thermometer is helpful, but I've done this many times with a meat thermometer.

4. Meanwhile, line a pan with parchment paper and dust with the powdered sugar or arrowroot, or use a combo of both.

5. As soon as it reaches 240°F (115°C), remove the saucepan from the heat. Slowly pour the syrup into the bloomed gelatin.

6. Add the vanilla and cinnamon. Beat with a mixer for about 10 minutes until it suddenly turns to a marshmallow fluff.

7. Immediately pour the mixture onto your parchment paper–lined pan. Spread it evenly.

8. Sprinkle the top with more powdered sugar or arrowroot. Leave the marshmallows to sit overnight at room temperature.

9. Cut the marshmallows into your desired shape and size, and sprinkle them with more powdered sugar to prevent sticking.

10. Enjoy as a treat, in a cup of hot cocoa, or as part of a s'more!

My Mega Matcha

My husband is a coffee guy and spent years trying to get me to have a morning beverage with him when he woke up. I never really took to coffee, and there was never a tea or other beverage that stood out—until matcha hit the scene. The year matcha arrived as a trend, I kept hearing about the benefits and had to try it. I was not immediately on board with the strong earthy flavor, though it did grow on me.

Still, to this day, my daily drink is not a straight matcha. I add cinnamon and believe a pinch of salt makes everything taste better. Collagen also has many great health benefits, and it contributes to the rich creaminess of this concoction. Sometimes I add ½ teaspoon maca powder for a caramel flavor, a boost of energy, and hormonal support. And most important, my husband and I now both have something lovely to sip in the morning.

Yield: Serves 4

Ingredients:

¼ cup (59 ml) raw cream

⅛–¼ teaspoon Ceylon cinnamon (see note) or regular ground cinnamon

1 teaspoon (15 ml) coconut oil

1–2 tablespoons (15–30 ml) grass-fed collagen

1 heaping teaspoon high-quality ceremonial-grade matcha

1 teaspoon raw honey

Pinch of sea salt

Hot filtered water

1. In a quart-size (1-L) mason jar or heat-proof large glass, add all the ingredients except the water.

2. Add the hot water to reach 16 ounces (500 ml).

3. Use a whisk or hand frother to blend.

4. Pour into your favorite mug, and enjoy!

Note: *Ceylon cinnamon is like the king of cinnamon. It is known to improve blood quality and flow. It has been said to fight diabetes, infections, and viruses, and also has anti-inflammatory properties among many other reported benefits.*

Matcha is not only energizing, it also:

- Is high in antioxidants
- Is an excellent source of prebiotics
- Is energy without jitters or a crash
- Improves immune system function
- Is cancer fighting
- Is metabolism supportive
- Slows some aging processes
- Fights inflammation
- Supports brain health
- Supports heart health
- Is delicious

Gelatin Gummies

Gummies were intimidating to me to make before I knew how to use gelatin. The molds do add a bit of complexity, but I encourage you to try sometime if you have kids around because they just love them and it can be a fun activity. When I make the shapes, I'll err on the heavy side for gelatin to make it easier for them to pop out. Use what you have on hand, and don't be afraid to mix juices.

Yield: Makes enough for an
  8 × 8-inch (20 × 20-cm) glass pan

Ingredients:
Coconut oil, for greasing
3 cups (720 ml) liquid, such as juice
  (see note)
9–12 tablespoons (83–111 g)
  unflavored gelatin
Raw honey or maple syrup, to taste
Pinch of sea salt

Note: *Use the greater amount of unflavored gelatin if pouring into molds for a firmer gummy.*

Gelatin and Collagen

Traditionally people ate more nose to tail, and it is nice to see some enthusiasm returning for eating this way. Until everyone embraces it though, most people aren't getting much collagen and gelatin. This recipe is a super fun way to get a little more in your diet.

1. Grease an 8 × 8-inch (20 × 20-cm) glass pan or silicone molds with coconut oil.

2. In a large pot off the heat, combine the liquid with the gelatin. Let the gelatin bloom, without mixing, 3 to 5 minutes. When the gelatin is ready, it'll be bumpy and look like a brain.

3. Place the pot over low heat, and cook for 3 to 5 minutes until the gelatin dissolves. Sweeten with honey to taste, and add a pinch of salt.

4. Carefully pour the mixture into the pan or molds. Transfer it carefully to the refrigerator to chill for a couple hours until the gummies are firm.

Note: *Some juice combo/liquid options:*

Sweet + Tart: 1 cup (237 ml) each: orange juice, tart cherry juice, and cranberry juice

Pina Colada: 1 cup (237 ml) coconut cream and 2 cups (473 ml) pineapple juice

Orange Creamsicle: 2 cups (473 ml) orange juice and 1 cup (237 ml) coconut cream or heavy cream

sweets and sips

Quick Chia Jam

If you're looking for an alternative to sugary, store-bought jams, this is, um, the jam! Yes, you are in the driver's seat: You control the sugar content, and there's certainly no questionable ingredients like high-fructose corn syrup. In our house, we pretty much always have frozen mixed berries or strawberries, so that's what I usually make. But I've made this with all sorts of fruit with great results. In fact, when I tried it with frozen mango, it made me wonder why you don't see more mango jam on the shelf!

Note: *The chia creates its own little gel so it binds together and thickens up like a traditional jam while adding a bit more nourishment—lots of fiber, protein, and omegas!*

Yield: Makes 2 cups

Ingredients:

2 cups (473 ml) fresh or frozen fruit of choice, such as berries, mango, and pineapple

Optional: 1 tablespoon (15 ml) raw honey, maple syrup, or date syrup

2 tablespoons (30 g) chia seeds

Pinch of sea salt

1. If you're using frozen fruit, place it in a small pot over medium-low heat. Cook it until it's soft and mushy. Stir it occasionally, and if it's too chunky for your taste, mash it a bit, using a wooden spoon to press the fruit against the side of the pot. Turn off the heat, and remove the pot from the burner.

2. Mix in the sweetener (if using), chia seeds, and salt, stirring well to combine. Let the mixture cool in the pot, then transfer it to a storage container and refrigerate.

3. Enjoy the chia jam on on toast, in a yogurt parfait, in a PBJ, or any way you like!

How to Store: *The jam keeps for 1 week when refrigerated in an airtight container. Ours never lasts that long because it's too yummy! I haven't tried freezing any; if you have, please let me know how that works out!*

Honey Lemonade

I must have made lemonade with honey a dozen times, but I can still remember the day I crafted a big batch of this and put it in a beverage dispenser. (My husband was working with his dad building us our Shed-Cetera!) The reason I remember it so vividly is it was the first time I used honey and didn't think to myself "this tastes like honey more than lemonade." It's subtle, and I think the ratio is just right. And you won't notice the pinch of salt either, but it will make it even better.

Yield: Makes 1 gallon (3.8 L)

Ingredients:
10 cups (2.4 L) filtered water
2 or more cups (480 ml) fresh
   lemon juice (see note)
1 cup (237 ml) raw honey (Use
   local honey if you can get it.)
Pinch of sea salt

1. Place all the ingredients in a large container, such as a pitcher or two 64-ounce (1.9-L) mason jars with lids.

2. Stir to combine, or be extra like me and use an immersion blender.

3. Chill and serve.

Note: *Add more fresh lemon juice if you enjoy a tart lemonade. I use 2¼ to 2½ cups (540 to 600 ml).*

Cold Brew Coffee
with Cleaner Creamer

I don't drink coffee, but this is a hit here for my coffee-loving husband. I added a little special touch with creamer flavors, and he now happily declares it's better than his favorite order-out. Use your favorite coffee, but don't expect it to taste the same if you've never made cold brew before—it is way smoother and the aroma is different. The creamers here are some of his favorites, but you can add any spices or flavors you want to try to this base. And you'll feel great using them compared to the store-bought flavored creamers, which are notorious for containing natural flavors, preservatives, and thickeners.

Yield: Makes 4 cups

Ingredients:

1 cup (around 20 g) whole
   coffee beans

4 cups (960 ml) filtered water

Optional Add-Ins:

½ teaspoon ground cinnamon or
   pumpkin spice

Optional, for Serving:

Flavored Creamers (recipes follow)

1. Coarsely grind the whole beans. In a container, add the ground beans to the filtered water. I use a 64-ounce (1.9-L) mason jar. If using, stir in the spice.

2. Cover and store in the refrigerator for 8 to 24 hours.

3. Set a fine-mesh strainer over a batter bowl or large mixing bowl. Lay an organic flour-sack towel, nut bag, or tea towel over the strainer. Pour the coffee through. Pull up the sides of the towel, then give it a good squeeze to get out every drop.

4. Carefully pour the coffee from the bowl into glasses or mugs. Serve with flavored creamer or milk, if you like.

Tip: *Put your grounds in your compost or garden, or use them to make a body scrub!*

How to Store: *The coffee will keep for a few days in the fridge. You can also freeze it in ice cube trays to add to iced coffee drinks.*

continued on following page

sweets and sips

Vanilla Bean Coconut Creamer

Clean ingredients and so yum! Drizzle this into your coffee or tea, or use it to top your yogurt bowl or fruit or desserts. It gets extra thick and creamy once refrigerated.

Yield: Makes about 1¾ cups

Ingredients:

1 can (13½ ounces, or 400 ml) unsweetened coconut cream

1 teaspoon vanilla bean powder or vanilla extract

1 tablespoon (14 g) coconut sugar or your favorite sweetener

Pinch of sea salt

Dash of ground cinnamon

1. Using a blender, whisk, or immersion blender, combine all the ingredients until well blended.

2. Pour into an airtight container, then refrigerate it until cold. This will keep for about 1 week in the fridge. (If it lasts that long!)

Pumpkin Spice Creamer

Live your best autumny life. Add this to your coffee, hot cocoa, matcha, or whatever you wanna add some pumpkin pie creaminess to. You can whip it after refrigerating a full day to make a pumpkin spice whipped cream even.

Yield: Makes about 1½ cups

Ingredients:

1 can (13½ ounces, or 400 ml) unsweetened coconut cream

1 teaspoon pumpkin pie spice

1 teaspoon coconut sugar or any sweetener you like

½ teaspoon vanilla extract

Pinch of sea salt

1. Using a blender, whisk, or immersion blender, combine all the ingredients until well blended.

2. Pour into an airtight container, then refrigerate it until cold. This creamer keeps for about 1 week or so—if you don't guzzle it all sooner!

Healthier Hot Chocolate
(or Chocolate Milk)

I don't know about you, but I have a nostalgia for the hot chocolate I had as a child, even if it was nearly always from a packet. Because most of those packets contain ingredients I don't like, and they don't have enough chocolate flavor, I started digging into making a better mix. You may not get the rush of opening a packet, but I'm happy to say that with ingredients most likely already in your pantry and about ten seconds of your time, you will soon be sipping on a much better hot chocolate. Scale the recipe as needed to serve everyone!

Yield: Serves 1

Ingredients:

1 cup (237 ml) raw milk

1 tablespoon (6 g) cacao powder (see note)

1 tablespoon (15 ml) maple syrup

Pinch of sea salt

Optional: ⅛ teaspoon ground cinnamon

1. In a large measuring cup, whisk or froth all the ingredients until well combined.

2. For chocolate milk, serve it immediately or chill it briefly in the fridge before enjoying. For hot chocolate, pour it into a medium pot, warm it on the stovetop over medium-low heat, and carefully pour into a mug.

Note: *Cocoa and cacao are not the same. Although both come from the cacao bean, cacao is typically raw or sometimes processed at very low temperatures. This helps the end product retain some incredible properties. Cacao is a powerful antioxidant, helping protect the body against toxins and free radicals. Up to 10 percent of the cacao is made up of antioxidants, making it more antioxidant-rich than even açai, goji, and blueberries. It's also rich in minerals including magnesium, iron, potassium, calcium, zinc, copper, and manganese. Cacao is also reported to improve mood, reduce blood pressure, lower risk of cardiovascular disease, and lower insulin resistance. Super. Food.*

Cocoa powder is cacao that has been heated at high temperatures and is highly processed. This reduces the healthy benefits of the product greatly: Enzymes and nutritional content are reduced significantly. The end product is slightly sweeter, but no longer such a superfood.

Resources

A Little Less Toxic: My website has all of these products and brands with links listed plus loads of discounts and more, so be sure to go over and visit. www.alittlelesstoxic.com

My Amazon shop, where many of these items and more are linked: amazon.com/shop/alittlelesstoxic

Kitchen

Aarke: Premium sparkling water maker, aarke.us

All Clad: Stainless steel bakeware, cookware, and tools, all-clad.com

Almond Cow: Machine for making nut milk, almondcow.co

AquaTru: Countertop water filtration system, aquatruwater.com

AWG Bakery: Favorite grain-free breads made with real food ingredients, awgbakery.com

Ball: Mason jars with lids, newellbrands.com

Bink: My personal favorite glass water bottle with protective silicone sleeve, binkmade.com

Bissell: Steam mop for floors, bissell.com

Bon Ami: A nontoxic cleaner, bonami.com

Clearly Filtered: Water purifying systems, clearlyfiltered.com

Ecover: Dishwasher soap, ecover.com

Field Co.: Cast-iron skillets, fieldcompany.com

Greenfield Water Solutions: Structured water filters, greenfield water.com

Hu Chocolate: Chocolate bars, gems, chips, and hunks, hukitchen.com

Instant Pot Pressure Cooker: My most used kitchen appliance, instanthome.com

Kion: Coffee, protein bars, and supplements, getkion.com

Le Creuset: Cast-iron Dutch oven, lecreuset.com

Life Factory: Glass baby bottles, and water bottles, lifefactory.com

Lovebird Cereal: 100% real food cereals, organic, grain-free, no refined sugars, lovebirdfoods.com

Mama Meals: Frozen, organic, and nourishing meals to new moms based on ancient traditions, mama-meals.com

Mamma Mangia: Wood cutting boards, mammamangia.com

Masa Chips: Tortilla chips made with corn, tallow, and salt, without any seed oil, masachips.com

Mountain Rose Herbs: Herbs, teas, and oils, mountainroseherbs.com

Organifi: Plant-based superfoods, organifishop.com

Our Place: The Always Pan, fromourplace.ca

Paleovalley: A range of organic and Paleo-friendly products, such as coffee, olive oil, beef tallow, pork sticks, and supergreens, paleovalley.com

Pasture Bird: Chickens that live on fresh pasture; eat bugs, grains, grass, and legumes; and are moved daily to improve soil health. They are non-GMO, antibiotic-free, and have higher vitamin, mineral, and fatty acid content than traditional chicken, pasturebird.com

Pique: Quality, third-party tested teas, piquelife.com

Planet Box: Stainless lunch boxes for kids, planetbox.com

Primal Pastures: Premium pastured meats, primalpastures.com

Pyrex: Glass storage, batter bowl, pyrexhome.com

Redmond: Seasonings, toothpaste, and electrolytes, redmond.life

SaniTru: Multipurpose disinfectant kit, sanitru.com

Shark: Vacuum with a HEPA filter, sharkclean.com

Shun: Fancy, high-end kitchen knives of my dreams, shun.kaiusa.com

Siete: Heritage-inspired recipes and products made with better-for-you ingredients, sietefoods.com

Skout Organic: Snack bars for kids and adults, skoutorganic.com

Stasher: Food-grade silicone storage bags, stasherbag.com

Thrive Market: Online grocery pantry staples, cleaning products, etc., thrivemarket.com

Tramontina: Stainless steel pots and pans, tramontina.com

Truly Free Home: Nontoxic cleaning products, trulyfreehome.com

Vitamix: Efficient blender we use daily, vitamix.com/us/en_us

Wild Pastures: Delivers meat from regenerative American family farms to your doorstep for less. Customize your order, choose from grass-fed and pasture-raised beef, pork, chicken, and wild-caught seafood, wildpastures.com

Wusthof: Knife-block set, wusthof.com

Yeti: Stainless steel drinkware, coolers of all sizes, yeti.com

Yonanas: Turns frozen fruit into a yummy dessert fast, yonanas.com

Others

Ashley Smith: Helps achieve less mealtime stress and more feeding success. A pediatric dietitian nutritionist and mom of three, she shares expert advice on pediatric feeding topics such as picky eating, age-appropriate food ideas for infants on, mealtime organization tips, and more, www.veggiesandvirtue.com

Amy Williams, NTP: Helps people restore and reach optimal health through eating, environment, and extras. Swap indexes with helpful guidance for better choice foods and more. amymigdalia.com

Bethany Ugarte: Overcame life-threatening IBS and offers great digestive health recipes, tips, and insights! Author of *Digest This: The 21-Day Gut Reset Plan to Conquer Your IBS*, lilsipper.com

Brittany Williams: Lost 125 pounds in one year by focusing on home-cooked, real food. Shares wonderful recipes and ways to make real food fun, approachable, delicious, and nourishing. Author of the Instant Loss Cookbook Series and her memoir, Dear Body, instantloss.com

Brittyn Coleman: Registered dietitian, autism nutrition expert, and the creator of the Nourishing Autism Collective. Helps parents of kids on the autism spectrum looking to improve their child's nutrition, expand their diet, and help them feel their best and thrive. autismdietician.com

Dr. Ana Maria Temple: Dr. Temple is a pediatrician specializing in children's wellness and has a focus on overcoming eczema holistically. Author of *Healthy Kids in an Unhealthy World,* dranamaria.com

Dr. Elisa Song: A leading holistic pediatrician and mama of two, she educates on how to integrate natural and conventional treatments for your whole family. Author of *Healthy Kids, Happy Kids: An Integrative Pediatrician's Guide to Whole Child Resilience,* healthykidshappykids.com

Dr. Josh Axe, DNM, DC, CNS, has great information on all things health and nutrition, and provides some great recipes as well. draxe.com

Dr. Mark Hyman: A best-selling author, a leading expert in functional medicine, and a popular speaker on topics such as nutrition, health, and wellness. drhyman.com

Dr. Organic Mommy: Natasha Beck, M.P.H., Psy.D in pediatric neuropsychology, is a wealth of knowledge on raising kids well and living less toxic. She shares many better-choice food swaps and ideas as well as nontoxic items for the kitchen and packable lunches and more. drorganicmommy.com

Dr. William Bulsiewicz: AKA Dr. B. Board certified gastroenterologist specializing in the relationship between our gut microbiome and our health. Author of *Fiber Fueled* and *The Fiber Fueled Cookbook*, theplantfedgut.com

Fallon Danae: A kitchen creative with wonderful recipes, resources, tips, and support to find healing through food freedom. Such an encouragement for making food at home, simply and deliciously. She has recipes, resources, tips, and support to find healing through food freedom. fallonstable.com

Homegrown Education: Offers a wide variety of resources, including breakfast and dinner meal plans, kids' resources, a free raw dairy guide, and a free beginner's sourdough guide. homegrowneducation.org

Iliriana Balaj: Illiriana is a holistic health coach and certified personal trainer that inspires and educates about using real food to feel and perform our best. She has an online shop filled with goods that make it easier to find and buy less toxic products for the kitchen, home, and life. livehealthillie.com

Just Ingredients: Karalynne is always offering a better option for conventional brands and has even gone on to create her own products with only the best ingredients. justingredients.us

Plateful Health: Dr. Vivian Chen, M.D., is board-certified in the UK in internal medicine and family practice, and is a brilliant doctor and an incredible resource on nontoxic living and health. Her Detox Right course is the best I've ever seen and so full of helpful information you won't want to miss. platefulhealth.com

Sandy Leibowitz: Sandy is a professionally trained chef and home cook that teaches cooking skills and techniques in easy-to-apply ways so anyone can make great meals at home. plantainsandchallah.com

Shandy Laskey, M.A., CCC-SLP, FNTP: Holistic nutrition, feeding, and development coaching for naturally minded parents of children with complex picky eating and developmental conditions. www.speakingof healthandwellness.com

The Family Food Project: Kayla shares helpful tips, tricks, and ideas for feeding your family delicious, fun, and nourishing meals. thefamilyfoodproject.com

Vani Hari: Vani is a pioneer of the food revolution space. Food activist and best-selling author. She exposes harmful ingredients in food and offers healthy alternatives, recipes, and products. foodbabe.com

Helpful Sites and Apps

Think Dirty: Encourages ingredient conscious consumers to choose safe products by checking the rating and showing potential dangers of certain ingredients. thinkdirtyapp.com

EWG: Helps provide research and data in order to make informed decisions about the products and brands you use. ewg.org/ foodscores

LocalFats.com: An independent project built to connect you with restaurants that are serving real food and help us search for restaurants by the cooking oil they use. localfats.com

MadeSafe: A nonprofit organization that certifies safe products made without toxic chemicals. madesafe.org

Seed Oil Scout: An app enabling the community of conscious diners to map out restaurants that care for their customers by cooking with healthy oils. seedoilscout.com

Yuka: Scans and analyzes labels in the blink of an eye so you can learn at a glance which products are good for you and which ones you should avoid. yuka.io/en

At the time of this writing these are the brands and products that I love and use in my home and would recommend to friends and others.

Be mindful to continue to read ingredients labels on everything, even on the products and brands that you've come to trust and love, because they can change. Sometimes brands get bought by bigger companies who don't have the same concern for what goes into the products. Sometimes brands change formulation, and it's important to continue to read and be informed about what you're inviting into your home.

In compliance with the FTC guidelines, please assume the following for any references included in this book.

Many of the links to products here are affiliate links. This means I receive a commission from sales at no additional cost to you. Most times the cost is actually lower for you as I'm able to provide discounts! I only affiliate myself with either companies that I genuinely buy from already, or products that I have tried and continue to authentically use. All of my affiliate links are to products that I personally use, support, and recommend to my friends and family. Affiliating myself with a company I love allows me to support brands that I value and recommend. I also often get to help you save on the products I use and love. When you shop using my links, you're also supporting me as I sometimes earn a commission from purchases made using my link.

Acknowledgments

I'd like to first acknowledge all the cooks and chefs who inspired me and instructed me as a young adult—often on TV or social media. I have learned most of what I know about cooking from watching my favorite chefs and home cooks, many also without formal training, preparing meals from scratch on television shows. It inspired me, and it helped me to feel brave and confident enough to prepare more dishes myself at home. Seeing what helped you gain confidence and competence in your own kitchens lights my fire! We all sharpen each other.

To Damien: You are the best man I have ever known. Thank you for being mine. Breaking bread with you is always and forever my favorite. I have many more words I want to say to you about my appreciation, great respect, and admiration of the man you are in my life, in our family, and in this world. I'll tell you tonight. And every night the Lord blesses me with breath that I might continue to have the privilege of being yours.

To Ezekiel and Abigail: I love making food with you. I love enjoying meals together with you. I love feeding you. I love seeing you create your own recipes and master them. You are the Healthier Home Cooks of the now and the future, and you bring my heart so much cheer. I love you.

To Amy Nelsen: You technically made my first cookbook when you took every single one of the recipes I had ever shared online and made them into the most beautiful book so I could stop relying on the internet to cook my own recipes. It is a gift I will treasure always. Then you encouraged me to do the work to make this one come to life, and you held my hand and my heart every step of the way. I love doing life with you. I love doing ALLT with you. I love you. Thank you.

To Dave Nelsen: You may be an unofficial member of the tiny official team here, but you are a critical cog in the machine. One of the earliest and most sincere encouragers, and one of the most constant too. Thank you for being my friend. Thank you for sharing your bride with me. We talk entirely too much and, yet, it's never quite enough. I always appreciate your authentic food and product reviews, and more than that, I appreciate your authentic friendship. Damien and I are so blessed by our friendship with you all. Team Nelsen, forever.

To my mama: No one I know cooks like you. You make meals magical and do it so simply. You make nourishing foods taste and feel decadent. I am forever inspired by you for so many reasons. Your craft in the kitchen is up high on that list. Thank you for fighting for me, fueling me, and furthering my passions.

To my Mommy-in-Love Patty and Dad-in-Love Frank and the full Holman/Muller crew: Joining around the table with you all is one of my favorite things in this world. The meal is always wonderful, but the company is superior. Life with you is a blessing, "straight up!"

To Barbara and Dale St. John: You welcomed me at your family table more times than I can count. It taught me the value and power of a shared family meal around the table. I have so many memories from that table. You have blessed my life in countless ways, and I am forever grateful for you.

To my treasured friends and family who have faithfully held the secret of this book as well as held me along the way: You keep me going, and you bring me tremendous joy. You are the salt of the earth, and you season my life with goodness.

To the team at Quarto, most notably Thom O'Hearn: Thank you for the opportunity, the encouragement, and the support to make this labor of love come to life. I'm so glad I decided to consider that initial email years ago. You are doing good work, and I'm thankful to get to work with you.

To my wonderful team that made my recipes look so beautiful: Monica, Jill, and Kayla. Wow. I didn't know I could tear up so many times looking at meals I've prepared countless times myself. The way you crafted them and captured them is such an art. You are truly gifted. Thank you for sharing your gifts and talents with me and the world.

To Justin and Jill Scarpetti: You let me take over and utilize your beautiful kitchen once again. You created such a warm and gorgeous space, and it helped make this book extra special. You make everything you touch more lovely, including the world and the lives of others. Especially mine. Thank you for your unwavering friendship and generosity.

To the *A Little Less Toxic* community I'm so honored to be with online: It is because you have joined me in caring about and sharing about these things that I have this opportunity. I am so grateful for you. Thank you.

To every brand making less toxic products, and especially those I've come to know on a personal level: Your work matters. Your mission is important. You're making a difference. Thank you for your tireless work and commitment to making food and products that help people. I am so grateful for you.

To my good and gracious God: You are my daily bread. You could have made food bland and boring, yet you made it beautiful, delicious, and powerful, with infinite flavor combinations and unending ways to enjoy it. Thank you for helping me to appreciate the beauty of your creation and plan for our fuel.

To the one who is reading this right now: Together, we are taking back our health. We're bringing back shared meals. We're making food that fuels fun again. We're reshaping the food industry. Together, we have greater impact. Thank you for taking this journey with me. Thank you for caring and for allowing my words and recipes to be a part of your process.

Like the sign in my kitchen says, "Cook. Nourish. Enjoy."

a healthier home cook

About the Author

Shawna Holman, best-selling author of *A Healthier Home* and founder of A Little Less Toxic, is a mother, a wife, and a dedicated teacher. After battling life-altering health issues, Shawna was determined to find long-lasting and healthy solutions rather than harmful quick fixes. Once she began her journey toward making radical health improvements through small life changes, she soon began taking family, friends, and then fans and followers along for the ride. By seeking out, implementing, and sharing her life transformation, Shawna motivates her audience to support their health and healing through sustainable, realistic, and mindful lifestyle changes. Since healing herself and finding solace in creating a healthy home environment, Shawna is intent on sharing her story and helping those looking to live life A Little Less Toxic. Find her online at alittlelesstoxic.com.

Dedication

This book is dedicated to the *A Little Less Toxic* community. Without you, it would not exist. God blessed me by connecting me in some way to each of you precious souls. You cook my recipes, and it brings me immense joy to see you and your families enjoying the same nourishing meals my family love. It lights my fire to know that my sharing inspires you to make more food with your own hands. You have inspired me and encouraged me right back more than I can express with written word. I'm so grateful for you. From my kitchen and my heart to yours, this book is for you.

Index